Bilingual

VISUAL

dictionary

Bilingual

dictionary

Previously published as part of
5-Language Visual Dictionary

DK | Penguin
Random
House

Senior Editor Angeles Gavira
Senior Art Editor Ina Stradins
DTP Designers Sunil Sharma, Balwant Singh,
Harish Aggarwal, John Goldsmid, Ashwani Tyagi
DTP Coordinator Pankaj Sharma
Production Controller Liz Cherry
Picture Researcher Anna Grapes
Managing Editor Liz Wheeler
Managing Art Editor Phil Ormerod
Category Publisher Jonathan Metcalf

Designed for Dorling Kindersley by WaltonCreative.com
Art Editor Colin Walton, assisted by Tracy Musson
Designers Peter Radcliffe, Earl Neish, Ann Cannings
Picture Research Marissa Keating

Language content for Dorling Kindersley by
g-and-w PUBLISHING
Managed by Jane Wightwick, assisted by Ana Bremón
Translation and editing by Christine Arthur
Additional input by Dr. Arturo Pretel, Martin Prill,
Frédéric Monteil, Meinrad Prill, Mari Bremón,
Oscar Bremón, Anunchi Bremón, Leila Gaafar

First American Edition, 2009
This edition published in the United States in 2015
by DK Publishing, 345 Hudson Street, New York,
New York 10014

Copyright © 2015 Dorling Kindersley Limited

A Penguin Random House Company
15 16 17 18 19 10 9 8 7 6 5 4 3 2
002 – 283035 – June/15

A catalog record for this book is available from the
Library of Congress.
ISBN: 978-1-4654-3630-6

DK books are available at special discounts when purchased
in bulk for sales promotions, premiums, fund-raising, or
educational use. For details, contact: DK Publishing Special
Markets, 345 Hudson Street, New York, New York 10014
SpecialSales@dk.com

Printed and bound in China
All images © Dorling Kindersley Limited
For further information see: www.dkimages.com

A WORLD OF IDEAS:
SEE ALL THERE IS TO KNOW

www.dk.com

table des matières
contents

42
la santé
health

146
sortir manger
eating out

252
le temps libre
leisure

à propos du
dictionnaire

about the dictionary

comment utiliser
ce livre

how to use this book

I O

les gens

people

28

l'apparence

appearance

56

la maison

home

92

les services

services

I02

les courses

shopping

I I6

la nourriture

food

I60

l'étude

study

I70

le travail

work

I92

le transport

transportation

2I8

les sports

sports

278

l'environnement

environment

302

l'information

reference

324

index

index

360

remerciements

acknowledgments

à propos du dictionnaire

Il est bien connu que les illustrations nous aident à comprendre et retenir l'information. Fondé sur ce principe, ce dictionnaire bilingue richement illustré présente un large éventail de vocabulaire courant et utile dans deux langues européennes.

Le dictionnaire est divisé de façon thématique et couvre en détail la plupart des aspects du monde quotidien, du restaurant au gymnase, de la maison au lieu de travail, de l'espace au monde animal. Vous y trouverez également des mots et expressions supplémentaires pour la conversation et pour enrichir votre vocabulaire.

Il s'agit d'un outil de référence essentiel pour tous ceux qui s'intéressent aux langues – pratique, stimulant et d'emploi facile.

Quelques points à noter
Les deux langues sont toujours présentées dans le même ordre – français et anglais.

Les noms sont donnés avec leurs articles définis qui indiquent leur genre (masculin ou féminin) et leur nombre (singulier ou pluriel):

la graine   **les amendes**
seed   almonds

Les verbes sont indiqués par un (v), par exemple:

récolter • harvest (v)

Chaque langue a également son propre index à la fin du livre. Vous pourrez y vérifier un mot dans n'importe laquelle des deux langues et vous serez renvoyé au(x) numéro(s) de(s) page(s) où il figure. Le genre est indiqué par les abréviations suivantes:

m = masculin
f = féminin

about the dictionary

The use of pictures is proven to aid understanding and the retention of information. Working on this principle, this highly-illustrated bilingual dictionary presents a large range of useful current vocabulary in two European languages.

The dictionary is divided thematically and covers most aspects of the everyday world in detail, from the restaurant to the gym, the home to the workplace, outer space to the animal kingdom. You will also find additional words and phrases for conversational use and for extending your vocabulary.

This is an essential reference tool for anyone interested in languages – practical, stimulating, and easy-to-use.

A few things to note
The two languages are always presented in the same order – French and English.

Nouns are given with their definite articles reflecting the gender (masculine or feminine) and number (singular or plural), for example:

la graine   **les amendes**
seed   almonds

Verbs are indicated by a (v) after the English—for example:

récolter • harvest (v)

Each language also has its own index at the back of the book. Here you can look up a word in either of the two languages and be referred to the page number(s) where it appears. The gender is shown using the following abbreviations:

m = masculine
f = feminine

comment utiliser ce livre

Que vous appreniez une nouvelle langue pour les affaires, le plaisir ou pour préparer vos vacances, ou encore si vous espérez élargir votre vocabulaire dans une langue qui vous est déjà familière, ce dictionnaire sera pour vous un outil d'apprentissage précieux que vous pourrez utiliser de plusieurs manières.

Lorsque vous apprenez une nouvelle langue, recherchez les mots apparentés (mots qui se ressemblent dans différentes langues) et les faux amis (mots qui se ressemblent mais ont des significations nettement différentes). Par exemple, l'anglais a importé des autres langues européennes de nombreux termes désignant la nourriture mais, en retour, exporté des termes employés dans le domaine de la technologie et de la culture populaire.

Activités pratiques d'apprentissage
• Lorsque vous vous déplacez dans votre maison, au travail ou à l'université, essayez de regarder les pages qui correspondent à ce contexte. Vous pouvez ensuite fermer le livre, regarder autour de vous et voir combien d'objets vous pouvez nommer.
• Forcez-vous à écrire une histoire, une lettre ou un dialogue en employant le plus de termes possibles choisis dans une page. Ceci vous aidera à retenir le vocabulaire et son orthographe. Si vous souhaitez pouvoir écrire un texte plus long, commencez par des phrases qui incorporent 2 à 3 mots.
• Si vous avez une mémoire très visuelle, essayez de dessiner ou de décalquer des objets du livre sur une feuille de papier, puis fermez le livre et inscrivez les mots sous l'image.
• Une fois que vous serez plus sûr de vous, choisissez des mots dans l'index de la langue étrangère et essayez de voir si vous en connaissez le sens avant de vous reporter à la page correspondante pour vérifier.

how to use this book

Whether you are learning a new language for business, pleasure, or in preparation for an overseas vacation, or are hoping to extend your vocabulary in an already familiar language, this dictionary is a valuable learning tool that you can use in a number of different ways.

When learning a new language, look for cognates (words that are alike in different languages) and "false friends" (words that look alike but carry significantly different meanings). You can also see where the languages have influenced each other. For example, English has imported many terms for food from other European languages but, in turn, exported terms used in technology and popular culture.

Practical learning activities
• As you move around your home, workplace, or school, try looking at the pages which cover that setting. You could then close the book, look around you, and see how many of the objects and features you can name.
• Challenge yourself to write a story, letter, or dialogue using as many of the terms on a particular page as possible. This will help you retain the vocabulary and remember the spelling. If you want to build up to writing a longer text, start with sentences incorporating 2–3 words.
• If you have a very visual memory, try drawing or tracing items from the book onto a piece of paper, then closing the book and filling in the words below the picture.
• Once you are more confident, pick out words in a foreign-language index and see if you know what they mean before turning to the relevant page to see if you were right.

les gens
people

le corps • body

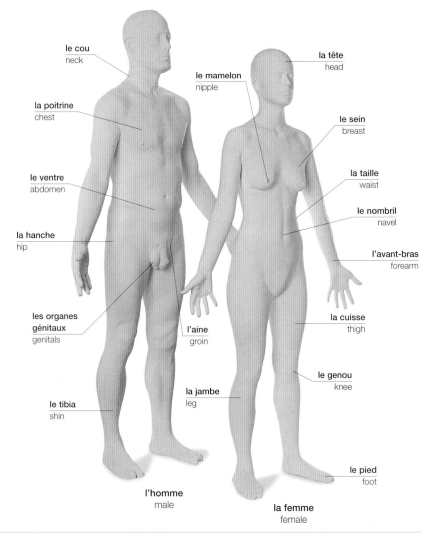

le cou
neck

la tête
head

le mamelon
nipple

la poitrine
chest

le sein
breast

le ventre
abdomen

la taille
waist

le nombril
navel

la hanche
hip

l'avant-bras
forearm

les organes
génitaux
genitals

l'aine
groin

la cuisse
thigh

la jambe
leg

le genou
knee

le tibia
shin

le pied
foot

l'homme
male

la femme
female

la nuque
nape of
neck

le dos
back

l'épaule
shoulder

l'aisselle
armpit

le bras
arm

le coude
elbow

le creux des reins
small of back

le poignet
wrist

la fesse
buttock

la main
hand

le mollet
calf

la cheville
ankle

le talon
heel

la femme
female

l'homme
male

le visage • face

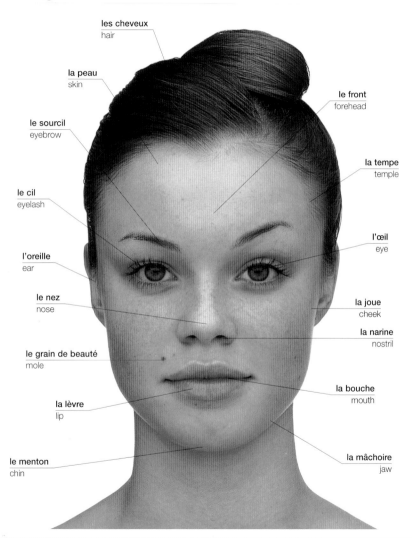

les cheveux
hair

la peau
skin

le sourcil
eyebrow

le cil
eyelash

l'oreille
ear

le nez
nose

le grain de beauté
mole

la lèvre
lip

le menton
chin

le front
forehead

la tempe
temple

l'œil
eye

la joue
cheek

la narine
nostril

la bouche
mouth

la mâchoire
jaw

la ride
wrinkle

la tache de rousseur
freckle

le pore
pore

la fossette
dimple

la main • hand

l'annulaire
ring finger

le majeur
middle finger

l'index
index finger

l'auriculaire
little finger

le poignet
wrist

la paume
palm

l'ongle
nail

la cuticule
cuticle

le nœud de l'articulation
knuckle

le pouce
thumb

le poing
fist

le pied • foot

le gros orteil
big toe

l'ongle du pied
toenail

l'avant-pied
ball

l'orteil
toe

le talon
heel

le petit orteil
little toe

le dos du pied
bridge

la plante du pied
sole

la cambrure
arch

la cheville
ankle

le cou-de-pied
instep

les muscles • muscles

le frontal
frontal

le pectoral
pectoral

le deltoïde
deltoid

le trapèze
trapezius

l'intercostal
intercostal

le dorsal
latissimus dorsi

le biceps
biceps

le triceps
triceps

les abdominaux
abdominals

le tendon
du jarret
hamstring

le fessier
buttock

les quadriceps
quadriceps

le tendon
d'Achille
Achilles tendon

les muscles
jumeaux
calf

le squelette • skeleton

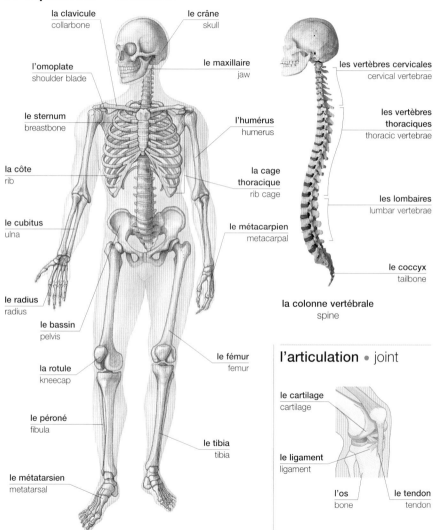

la clavicule
collarbone

le crâne
skull

l'omoplate
shoulder blade

le maxillaire
jaw

le sternum
breastbone

l'humérus
humerus

la côte
rib

la cage
thoracique
rib cage

le cubitus
ulna

le métacarpien
metacarpal

le radius
radius

le bassin
pelvis

la rotule
kneecap

le fémur
femur

le péroné
fibula

le tibia
tibia

le métatarsien
metatarsal

les vertèbres cervicales
cervical vertebrae

les vertèbres
thoraciques
thoracic vertebrae

les lombaires
lumbar vertebrae

le coccyx
tailbone

la colonne vertébrale
spine

l'articulation • joint

le cartilage
cartilage

le ligament
ligament

l'os
bone

le tendon
tendon

les organes internes • internal organs

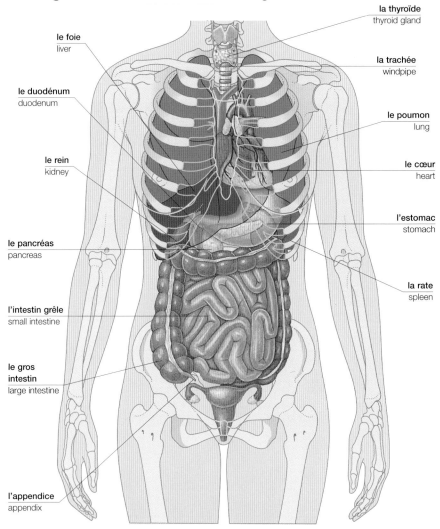

la thyroïde
thyroid gland

le foie
liver

la trachée
windpipe

le duodénum
duodenum

le poumon
lung

le rein
kidney

le cœur
heart

l'estomac
stomach

le pancréas
pancreas

la rate
spleen

l'intestin grêle
small intestine

le gros
intestin
large intestine

l'appendice
appendix

la tête • head

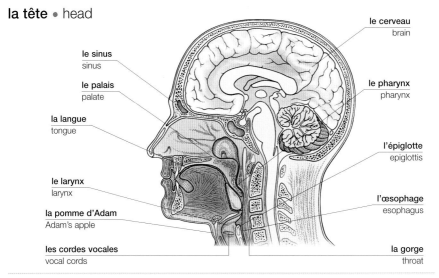

le cerveau
brain

le sinus
sinus

le palais
palate

la langue
tongue

le larynx
larynx

la pomme d'Adam
Adam's apple

les cordes vocales
vocal cords

le pharynx
pharynx

l'épiglotte
epiglottis

l'œsophage
esophagus

la gorge
throat

les systèmes du corps • body systems

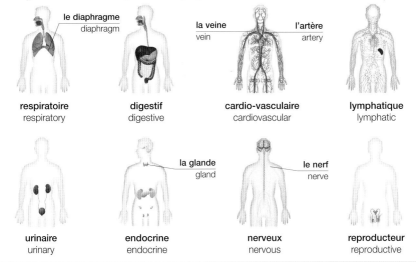

le diaphragme
diaphragm

la veine
vein

l'artère
artery

respiratoire
respiratory

digestif
digestive

cardio-vasculaire
cardiovascular

lymphatique
lymphatic

la glande
gland

le nerf
nerve

urinaire
urinary

endocrine
endocrine

nerveux
nervous

reproducteur
reproductive

les organes de reproduction • reproductive organs

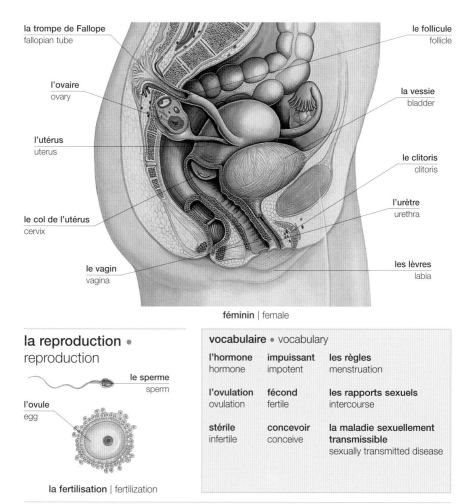

la trompe de Fallope
fallopian tube

le follicule
follicle

l'ovaire
ovary

la vessie
bladder

l'utérus
uterus

le clitoris
clitoris

l'urètre
urethra

le col de l'utérus
cervix

le vagin
vagina

les lèvres
labia

féminin | female

la reproduction • reproduction

le sperme
sperm

l'ovule
egg

la fertilisation | fertilization

vocabulaire • vocabulary

l'hormone hormone	**impuissant** impotent	**les règles** menstruation
l'ovulation ovulation	**fécond** fertile	**les rapports sexuels** intercourse
stérile infertile	**concevoir** conceive	**la maladie sexuellement transmissible** sexually transmitted disease

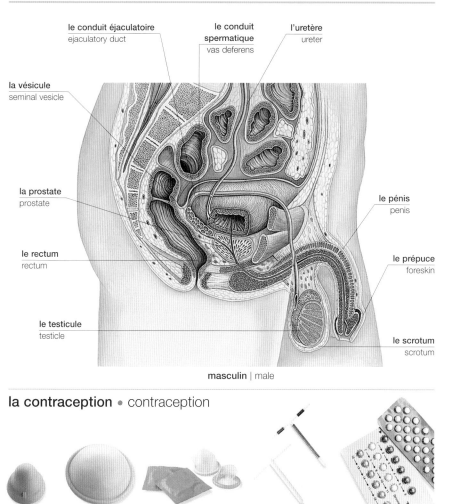

le conduit éjaculatoire
ejaculatory duct

le conduit
spermatique
vas deferens

l'uretère
ureter

la vésicule
seminal vesicle

la prostate
prostate

le pénis
penis

le rectum
rectum

le prépuce
foreskin

le testicule
testicle

le scrotum
scrotum

masculin | male

la contraception • contraception

**la cape
cervicale**
cervical cap

le diaphragme
diaphragm

le condom
condom

le stérilet
IUD

la pilule
pill

la famille • family

la grand-mère
grandmother

le grand-père
grandfather

l'oncle
uncle

la tante
aunt

le père
father

la mère
mother

le cousin
cousin

le frère
brother

la sœur
sister

la femme
wife

la belle-fille
daughter-in-law

le fils
son

la fille
daughter

le gendre
son-in-law

le petit-fils
grandson

la petite-fille
granddaughter

le mari
husband

vocabulaire • vocabulary

les parents relatives	**les parents** parents	**les petits-enfants** grandchildren	**la belle-mère** stepmother	**le beau-fils** stepson	**la génération** generation
les grands-parents grandparents	**les enfants** children	**le beau-père** stepfather	**la belle-fille** stepdaughter	**le/la partenaire** partner	**les jumeaux** twins

la belle-mère
mother-in-law

le beau-père
father-in-law

le beau-frère
brother-in-law

la belle-sœur
sister-in-law

la nièce
niece

le neveu
nephew

Mademoiselle
Miss

les titres • titles

Madame
Mrs.

Monsieur
Mr.

les stades • stages

le bébé
baby

l'enfant
child

le garçon
boy

la fille
girl

l'adolescente
teenager

l'adulte
adult

l'homme
man

la femme
woman

français • english

23

les relations • relationships

l'assistante
assistant

le chef
manager

l'associée
business
partner

l'employeur
employer

l'employée
employee

le collègue
colleague

le bureau | office

le voisin
neighbor

l'ami
friend

la connaissance
acquaintance

le correspondant
pen pal

le petit ami
boyfriend

la petite amie
girlfriend

le fiancé
fiancé

la fiancée
fiancée

le couple | couple

les fiancés | engaged couple

les émotions • emotions

le sourire
smile

heureux
happy

triste
sad

excité
excited

ennuyé
bored

surpris
surprised

effrayé
scared

le froncement
de sourcils
frown

fâché
angry

confus
confused

inquiet
worried

nerveux
nervous

fier
proud

confiant
confident

gêné
embarrassed

timide
shy

vocabulaire • vocabulary

consterné upset	**rire** laugh (v)	**soupirer** sigh (v)	**crier** shout (v)
choqué shocked	**pleurer** cry (v)	**s'évanouir** faint (v)	**bâiller** yawn (v)

les événements de la vie • life events

naître
be born (v)

commencer à l'école
start school (v)

se faire des amis
make friends (v)

obtenir sa licence
graduate (v)

trouver un emploi
get a job (v)

tomber amoureux
fall in love (v)

se marier
get married (v)

avoir un bébé
have a baby (v)

le mariage | wedding

le divorce
divorce

l'enterrement
funeral

vocabulaire • vocabulary

le baptême christening	**mourir** die (v)
la bar-mitsvah bar mitzvah	**faire son testament** make a will (v)
l'anniversaire de mariage anniversary	**l'acte de naissance** birth certificate
émigrer emigrate (v)	**le repas de noces** wedding reception
prendre sa retraite retire (v)	**le voyage de noces** honeymoon

les fêtes • celebrations

la fête
birthday party

la carte
card

le cadeau
present

l'anniversaire
birthday

le Noël
Christmas

les fêtes •
festivals

la Pâque
Passover

le Nouvel An
New Year

le carnaval
carnival

le défilé
procession

le Ramadan
Ramadan

le ruban
ribbon

la fête de Thanksgiving
Thanksgiving

Pâques
Easter

la veille de la Toussaint
Halloween

la Diwali
Diwali

l'apparence
appearance

les vêtements d'enfants • children's clothing

le bébé • baby

la combinaison de neige
snowsuit

le tricot
de corps
bodysuit

le bouton-
pression
snap

la grenouillère
onesie

le pyjama
sleeper

la combinaison-short
romper

le bavoir
bib

les moufles
mittens

les chaussons
booties

la couche
éponge
cloth diaper

la couche jetable
disposable diaper

la culotte en
plastique
plastic pants

---

le petit enfant • toddler

le t-shirt
t-shirt

la salopette
overalls

le chapeau de
soleil
sun hat

le tablier
apron

le bermuda
shorts

la jupe
skirt

---

l'enfant • child

la robe
dress

la capuche
hood

le jean
jeans

les
sandales
sandals

l'été
summer

l'imperméable
raincoat

le sac à dos
backpack

le bouton
toggle

l'automne
fall

le duffel-coat
duffel coat

l'écharpe
scarf

l'anorak
parka

les bottes de
caoutchouc
rain boots

l'hiver
winter

la robe de
chambre
bathrobe

le logo
logo

les baskets
athletic
shoes

la chemise de nuit
nightgown

les pantoufles
slippers

les vêtements de nuit
nightwear

la tenue de foot
soccer uniform

le survêtement
jogging suit

les leggings
leggings

vocabulaire • vocabulary

la fibre naturelle
natural fiber

synthétique
synthetic

C'est lavable en machine?
Is it machine-washable?

C'est la bonne taille pour
deux ans?
Will this fit a two-year-old?

les vêtements pour hommes • men's clothing

le col
collar

la cravate
tie

la ceinture
belt

le revers
lapel

la boutonnière
buttonhole

la manchette
cuff

la poche
pocket

la veste
jacket

le pantalon
pants

le bouton
button

les chaussures en cuir
leather shoes

le costume
business suit

l'imperméable
raincoat

la doublure
lining

vocabulaire • vocabulary

le cardigan	les sous-vêtements	le manteau	court
cardigan	underwear	coat	short
le peignoir	le survêtement	long	
dressing gown	tracksuit	long	

Avez-vous ça en plus grand/petit?
Do you have this in a larger/smaller size?

Je peux l'essayer?
May I try this on?

le blazer
blazer

la veste de sport
sport coat

le gilet
vest

l'encolure en V
V-neck

le col rond
crew neck

le t-shirt
t-shirt

l'anorak
parka

le sweat-shirt
sweatshirt

la chemise
shirt

le jean
jeans

le pullover
sweater

le pyjama
pajamas

le tricot de corps
undershirt

les vêtements sport
casual wear

le short
shorts

le slip
briefs

le caleçon
boxer shorts

les chaussettes
socks

les vêtements pour femmes • women's clothing

la veste
jacket

la couture
seam

sans bretelles
strapless

sans manches
sleeveless

la manche
sleeve

long
ankle length

la jupe
skirt

la robe du soir
evening dress

la robe
dress

le chemisier
blouse

le pantalon
pants

l'ourlet
hem

à genou
knee-length

les chaussures
shoes

habillé
formal

décontracté
casual

la lingerie • lingerie

le peignoir
robe

le caraco
slip

la bretelle
strap

la camisole
camisole

la jarretelle
garter

la guêpière
bustier

le bas
stocking

le collant
pantyhose

le soutien-gorge
bra

le slip
panties

la chemise de nuit
nightgown

le mariage • wedding

le voile
veil

la dentelle
lace

le bouquet
bouquet

la traîne
train

la robe de mariée
wedding dress

vocabulaire • vocabulary

le corset corset	**ajusté** tailored
la jarretière garter	**dos-nu** halter neck
l'épaulette shoulder pad	**à armature** underwired
la ceinture waistband	**le soutien-gorge sport** sports bra

les accessoires • accessories

la boucle
buckle

le manche
handle

la casquette
cap

le chapeau
hat

le foulard
scarf

la ceinture
belt

la pointe
tip

le mouchoir
handkerchief

le nœud papillon
bow tie

l'épingle de cravate
tie-pin

les gants
gloves

le parapluie
umbrella

les bijoux • jewelry

le rang de perles
string of pearls

le pendentif
pendant

la broche
brooch

le bouton de manchette
cufflink

le maillon
link

le fermoir
clasp

la boucle d'oreille
earring

la bague
ring

la pierre
stone

le collier
necklace

la montre
watch

le bracelet
bracelet

la chaîne
chain

la boîte à bijoux | jewelry box

les sacs • bags

le portefeuille
wallet

le porte-monnaie
purse

le sac à bandoulière
shoulder bag

le fermoir
fastening

la bretelle
shoulder strap

les poignées
handles

le fourre-tout
duffel bag

la serviette
briefcase

le sac à main
handbag

le sac à dos
backpack

les chaussures • shoes

le lacet
lace

la languette
tongue

l'œillet
eyelet

la semelle
sole

la chaussure lacée
lace-up

le talon
heel

la botte
boot

le pataugas
hiking boot

la basket
athletic shoe

la tong
flip-flop

la chaussure de cuir
leather shoe

la chaussure à talon
high-heeled shoe

la chaussure compensée
wedge

la sandale
sandal

le mocassin
slip-on

la ballerine
pump

les cheveux • hair

le peigne
comb

peigner
comb (v)

la brosse
brush

brosser | brush (v)

la coiffeuse
hairdresser

le lavabo
sink

la cliente
client

laver | wash (v)

le peignoir
robe

rincer
rinse (v)

couper
cut (v)

sécher
blow-dry (v)

faire une mise en plis
set (v)

les accessoires • accessories

le
sèche-
cheveux
hairdryer

le shampoing
shampoo

l'après-shampoing
conditioner

le gel
gel

la laque
hairspray

le fer à friser
curling iron

les ciseaux
scissors

le serre-tête
hairband

le fer à lisser
hair straighteners

la pince à cheveux
bobby pin

les coiffures • styles

la queue de cheval ponytail	**la natte** braid	**le rouleau** French twist	**le chignon** bun	**les couettes** pigtails

au carré bob	**la coupe courte** crop	**frisé** curly	**la permanente** perm	**raide** straight

les racines
roots

les reflets highlights	**chauve** bald	**la perruque** wig

les couleurs • colors

blond blonde	**châtain** brunette	**auburn** auburn	**roux** red

noir black	**gris** gray	**blanc** white	**teint** dyed

---

vocabulaire • vocabulary

rafraîchir trim (v)	**gras** greasy
décrêper straighten (v)	**sec** dry
le coiffeur barber	**normal** normal
les pellicules dandruff	**le cuir chevelu** scalp
les fourches split ends	**l'élastique pour cheveux** hairband

---

la beauté • beauty

la teinture de cheveux
hair dye

le fard à
paupières
eye shadow

le mascara
mascara

l'eye-liner
eyeliner

le fard à joues
blush

le fond de teint
foundation

le rouge à lèvres
lipstick

le maquillage • makeup

le crayon à sourcils
eyebrow pencil

la brosse à sourcils
eyebrow brush

la pince à épiler
tweezers

le brillant à lèvres
lip gloss

le pinceau à lèvres
lip brush

le crayon à lèvres
lip liner

le pinceau
brush

le correcteur
concealer

le miroir
mirror

la poudre
face powder

la houppette
powder puff

le poudrier | compact

les soins de beauté • beauty treatments

le masque de beauté
face mask

le lit U.V.
sunbed

le soin du visage
facial

exfolier
exfoliate (v)

l'épilation
wax

la pédicurie
pedicure

la manucure • manicure

le dissolvant
nail polish remover

la lime à ongles
nail file

le vernis à ongles
nail polish

les ciseaux à ongles
nail scissors

le coupe-ongles
nail clippers

les accessoires de toilette • toiletries

le démaquillant
cleanser

le tonique
toner

la crème hydratante
moisturizer

l'autobronzant
self-tanning cream

le parfum
perfume

l'eau de toilette
cologne

vocabulaire • vocabulary

le teint complexion	gras oily	le bronzage tan
clair fair	sensible sensitive	le tatouage tattoo
foncé dark	hypoallergénique hypoallergenic	antirides anti-wrinkle
sec dry	le ton shade	les boules de coton cotton balls

la santé
health

la maladie • illness

la fièvre | fever

l'inhalateur
inhaler

le mal de tête
headache

le saignement de nez
nosebleed

la toux
cough

l'éternuement
sneeze

le rhume
cold

la grippe
flu

l'asthme
asthma

les crampes
cramps

la nausée
nausea

la varicelle
chickenpox

l'éruption
rash

vocabulaire • vocabulary

l'attaque stroke	**le diabète** diabetes	**l'eczéma** eczema	**le refroidissement** chill	**vomir** vomit (v)	**la diarrhée** diarrhea
la tension blood pressure	**l'allergie** allergy	**l'infection** infection	**le mal d'estomac** stomachache	**l'épilepsie** epilepsy	**la rougeole** measles
la crise cardiaque heart attack	**le rhume des foins** hayfever	**le virus** virus	**s'évanouir** faint (v)	**la migraine** migraine	**les oreillons** mumps

le médecin • doctor
la consultation • consultation

le médecin
doctor

la lampe de radio
X-ray viewer

l'ordonnance
prescription

la patiente
patient

l'infirmière
nurse

la balance
scale

le manchon
cuff

le tensiomètre électronique
electric blood pressure monitor

vocabulaire • vocabulary

le rendez-vous appointment	**l'inoculation** inoculation
le cabinet surgery	**le thermomètre** thermometer
la salle d'attente waiting room	**l'examen médical** medical examination

J'ai besoin de voir un médecin.
I need to see a doctor.

J'ai mal ici.
It hurts here.

la blessure • injury

l'écharpe
sling

la minerve
neck brace

l'entorse | sprain

la fracture
fracture

le coup du lapin
whiplash

la coupure
cut

l'écorchure
graze

la contusion
bruise

l'écharde
splinter

le coup de soleil
sunburn

la brûlure
burn

la morsure
bite

la piqûre
sting

vocabulaire • vocabulary

l'accident accident	l'hémorragie hemorrhage	l'empoisonnement poisoning	**Est-ce qu'il/elle va se remettre?** Will he/she be all right?
l'urgence emergency	l'ampoule blister	le choc électrique electric shock	**Où avez-vous mal?** Where does it hurt?
la blessure wound	la commotion cérébrale concussion	le traumatisme crânien head injury	**Appelez une ambulance s'il vous plaît.** Please call an ambulance.

les premiers secours • first aid

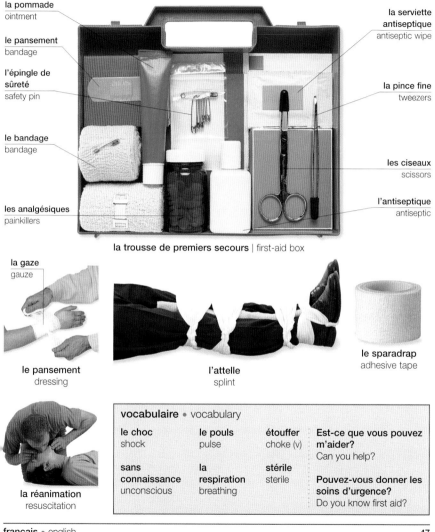

la pommade
ointment

le pansement
bandage

l'épingle de
sûreté
safety pin

le bandage
bandage

les analgésiques
painkillers

la serviette
antiseptique
antiseptic wipe

la pince fine
tweezers

les ciseaux
scissors

l'antiseptique
antiseptic

la trousse de premiers secours | first-aid box

la gaze
gauze

le pansement
dressing

l'attelle
splint

le sparadrap
adhesive tape

la réanimation
resuscitation

vocabulaire • vocabulary

le choc shock	**le pouls** pulse	**étouffer** choke (v)	**Est-ce que vous pouvez m'aider?** Can you help?
sans connaissance unconscious	**la respiration** breathing	**stérile** sterile	**Pouvez-vous donner les soins d'urgence?** Do you know first aid?

l'hôpital • hospital

le chirurgien
surgeon

la courbe
chart

l'analyse de sang
blood test

l'anesthésiste
anesthetist

l'injection
injection

l'infirmière
nurse

la salle d'opération
operating room

la radio
X-ray

le chariot
gurney

le bouton d'appel
call button

la scanographie
scan

la salle des urgences
emergency room

la salle
ward

la chaise roulante
wheelchair

---

vocabulaire • vocabulary

l'opération operation	**renvoyé** discharged	**les heures de visite** visiting hours	**la pédiatrie** children's ward	**le service de soins intensifs** intensive care unit
admis admitted	**la clinique** clinic	**la maternité** maternity ward	**la chambre privée** private room	**le malade en consultation externe** outpatient

---

les services • departments

l'O.R.L.
ENT (otolaryngology)

la cardiologie
cardiology

l'orthopédie
orthopedics

la gynécologie
gynecology

la kinésithérapie
physiotherapy

la dermatologíe
dermatology

la pédiatrie
pediatrics

la radiologie
radiology

la chirurgie
surgery

la maternité
maternity

la psychiatrie
psychiatry

l'ophtalmologie
ophthalmology

---

vocabulaire • vocabulary

la neurologie neurology	**l'urologie** urology	**l'endocrinologie** endocrinology	**la pathologie** pathology	**le résultat** result
l'oncologie oncology	**la chirurgie esthétique** plastic surgery	**l'orientation d'un patient** referral	**l'analyse** test	**le spécialiste** consultant

---

le dentiste • dentist

la dent • tooth

l'émail
enamel

la gencive
gum

le nerf
nerve

la racine
root

la prémolaire
premolar

l'incisive
incisor

la molaire
molar

la canine
canine

vocabulaire • vocabulary

la rage de dents	la fraise
toothache	drill
la plaque	le fil dentaire
plaque	dental floss
la carie	l'extraction
decay	extraction
le plombage	la couronne
filling	crown

la visite de contrôle • checkup

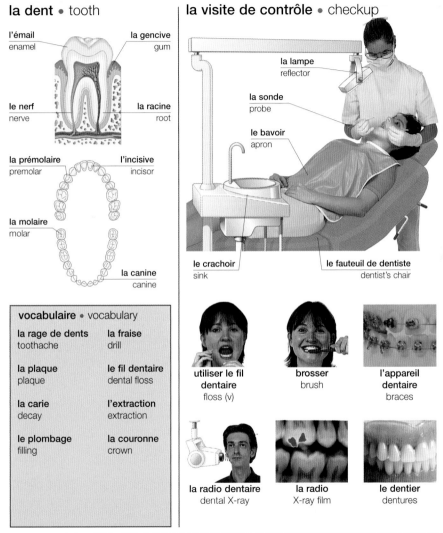

la lampe
reflector

la sonde
probe

le bavoir
apron

le crachoir
sink

le fauteuil de dentiste
dentist's chair

utiliser le fil dentaire
floss (v)

brosser
brush

l'appareil dentaire
braces

la radio dentaire
dental X-ray

la radio
X-ray film

le dentier
dentures

---

l'opticien • optometrist

l'étui
case

le verre
lens

la monture
frame

les lunettes
glasses

les lunettes de soleil
sunglasses

la solution nettoyante
cleaning fluid

la solution
désinfectante
disinfectant solution

l'étui à lentilles
lens case

l'examen de la vue | eye test

les lentilles de contact | contact lenses

l'œil • eye

le sourcil
eyebrow

la paupière
eyelid

le cil
eyelash

la pupille
pupil

l'iris
iris

la rétine
retina

le cristallin
lens

le nerf optique
optic nerve

la cornée
cornea

vocabulaire • vocabulary

la vue vision	**l'astigmatisme** astigmatism
la dioptrie diopter	**la presbytie** farsightedness
la larme tear	**la myopie** nearsightedness
la cataracte cataract	**bifocal** bifocal

la grossesse • pregnancy

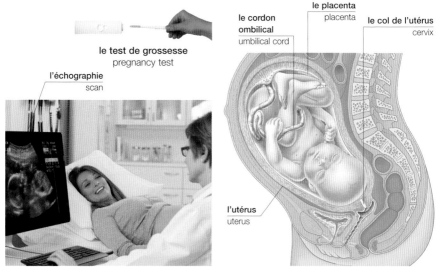

le test de grossesse
pregnancy test

l'échographie
scan

**le cordon
ombilical**
umbilical cord

le placenta
placenta

le col de l'utérus
cervix

l'utérus
uterus

les ultrasons | ultrasound

le fœtus | fetus

---

vocabulaire • vocabulary

l'ovulation ovulation	**prénatal** prenatal	**l'amniocentèse** amniocentesis	**la dilatation** dilation	**l'accouchement** delivery	**par le siège** breech
la conception conception	**l'embryon** embryo	**la contraction** contraction	**la péridurale** epidural	**la naissance** birth	**prématuré** premature
enceinte pregnant	**l'utérus** womb	**perdre les eaux** break water (v)	**l'épisiotomie** episiotomy	**la fausse couche** miscarriage	**le gynécologue** gynecologist
enceinte expecting	**le trimestre** trimester	**le liquide amniotique** amniotic fluid	**la césarienne** cesarean section	**les points de suture** stitches	**l'obstétricien** obstetrician

---

la naissance • childbirth

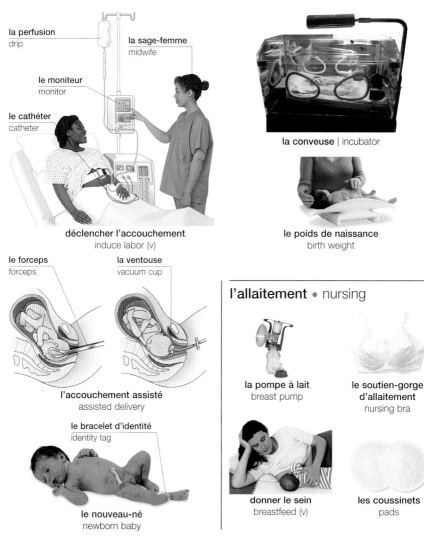

la perfusion
drip

la sage-femme
midwife

le moniteur
monitor

le cathéter
catheter

déclencher l'accouchement
induce labor (v)

la conveuse | incubator

le poids de naissance
birth weight

le forceps
forceps

la ventouse
vacuum cup

l'accouchement assisté
assisted delivery

le bracelet d'identité
identity tag

le nouveau-né
newborn baby

l'allaitement • nursing

la pompe à lait
breast pump

le soutien-gorge
d'allaitement
nursing bra

donner le sein
breastfeed (v)

les coussinets
pads

les thérapies alternatives • complementary therapy

le t-shirt
t-shirt

le tapis
mat

le yoga | yoga

le massage
massage

le shiatsu
shiatsu

la chiropractie
chiropractic

l'ostéopathie
osteopathy

la réflexologie
reflexology

la méditation
meditation

le conseiller
counselor

le reiki
reiki

l'acuponcture
acupuncture

la thérapie de groupe
group therapy

la médecine ayurvédique
ayurveda

l'hypnothérapie
hypnotherapy

les huiles essentielles
essential oils

l'herboristerie
herbalism

l'aromathérapie
aromatherapy

l'homéopathie
homeopathy

l'acupression
acupressure

la thérapeute
therapist

la psychothérapie
psychotherapy

---

vocabulaire • vocabulary

le supplément supplement	**la naturopathie** naturopathy	**la relaxation** relaxation	**l'herbe** herb
l'hydrothérapie hydrotherapy	**le feng shui** feng shui	**le stress** stress	**la guérison par cristaux** crystal healing

---

la maison
home

la maison • house

le toit
roof

la gouttière
gutter

la cheminée
chimney

le chien assis
dormer window

le mur
wall

la tuile
tile

l'avant-toit
eaves

le volet
shutter

le porche
porch

la fenêtre
window

l'agrandissement
addition

l'allée
sidewalk

la porte d'entrée
front door

vocabulaire • vocabulary

individuelle single-family	**le locataire** tenant	**le garage** garage	**la boîte aux lettres** mailbox	**l'alarme** burglar alarm	**louer** rent (v)
mitoyenne duplex	**la pavillon** ranch house	**le grenier** attic	**la lampe d'entrée** porch light	**la cour** courtyard	**le loyer** rent
la maison de deux étages townhouse	**le sous-sol** basement	**la chambre** room	**le propriétaire** landlord	**l'étage** floor	**attenante** terraced

l'entrée • entrance

l'appartement •
apartment

la main
courante
hand rail

le palier
landing

la rampe
banister

l'escalier
staircase

le vestibule
foyer

la sonnette
doorbell

le paillasson
doormat

le marteau de porte
door knocker

la clef
key

la chaîne de sûreté
door chain

la serrure
lock

le verrou
bolt

le balcon
balcony

l'immeuble
apartment building

l'interphone
intercom

l'ascenseur
elevator

les systèmes domestiques • internal systems

l'aile
blade

le ventilateur
fan

le radiateur
radiator

l'appareil de chauffage
space heater

le convecteur
convector heater

l'électricité • electricity

la mise à la terre
ground prong

le filament
filament

la broche
prong

neutre
neutral

sous tension
live

l'ampoule basse consommation
energy-saving bulb

la prise
plug

les fils
wires

vocabulaire • vocabulary

la tension voltage	**le fusible** fuse	**la prise de courant** outlet	**le courant continu** direct current	**la coupure de courant** power outage
l'ampère amp	**la boîte à fusibles** fuse box	**l'interrupteur** switch	**le transformateur** transformer	**le réseau d'électricité** household current
le courant power	**la génératrice** generator	**le courant alternatif** alternating current	**le compteur d'électricité** electric meter	

la plomberie • plumbing

l'arrivée
inlet

la sortie
outlet

la soupape de sûreté
pressure valve

l'isolation
insulation

le trop-plein
overflow pipe

le réservoir
tank

la chambre d'eau
water chamber

le robinet de purge
drain cock

le thermostat
thermostat

le brûleur à gaz
gas burner

la résistance
heating element

la chaudière
water heater

l'évier • sink

le robinet
faucet

la manette
lever

le joint
gasket

la conduite d'amenée
supply pipe

le robinet de sectionnement
shutoff valve

le tuyau d'écoulement
drain

le broyeur d'ordures
waste disposal unit

les W.-C. • toilet

la chasse-d'eau
tank

le flotteur
float ball

le siège
seat

le tuyau d'écoulement
waste pipe

la cuvette
bowl

l'enlèvement de déchets • waste disposal

la bouteille
bottle

le couvercle
lid

la pédale
pedal

la boîte à déchets recyclables
recycling bin

la poubelle
garbage can

la boîte de tri
sorting unit

les déchets bios
organic waste

le salon • living room

l'applique
wall light

la cheminée
fireplace

le plafond
ceiling

le vase
vase

le coussin
cushion

la lampe
lamp

la table
basse
coffee table

le canapé
sofa

le sol
floor

le cadre
frame

le tableau
painting

le rideau
curtain

le brise-bise
sheer curtain

le store vénitien
Venetian blind

le store
shade

la moulure
molding

le fauteuil
armchair

la bibliothèque
bookshelf

le canapé-lit
sofa bed

le tapis
rug

le bureau | study

la salle à manger • dining room

le poivre
pepper

le sel
salt

la table
table

la vaisselle
crockery

les couverts
cutlery

la chaise
chair

le dossier
back

le siège
seat

le pied
leg

---

vocabulaire • vocabulary

mettre la table set the table (v)	**(avoir) faim** hungry	**le déjeuner** lunch	**rassasié** full	**l'hôte** host	**Puis-je en reprendre un peu, s'il vous plaît?** Can I have some more, please?
servir serve (v)	**la nappe** tablecloth	**le dîner** dinner	**la portion** portion	**l'hôtesse** hostess	**Non merci, j'en ai eu assez.** I've had enough, thank you.
manger eat (v)	**le petit déjeuner** breakfast	**le set de table** placemat	**le repas** meal	**l'invité** guest	**C'était délicieux.** That was delicious.

---

la vaisselle et les couverts • crockery and cutlery

la cuiller à café
teaspoon

la grande tasse
mug

la tasse à thé
teacup

la tasse à café
coffee cup

l'assiette
plate

le bol
bowl

le verre à vin
wine glass

le verre
tumbler

la cafetière
cafetière

la théière
teapot

le pot
pitcher

le coquetier
egg cup

la verrerie
glassware

le rond de serviette
napkin ring

l'assiette à dessert
side plate

l'assiette plate
dinner plate

l'assiette à soupe
soup bowl

la cuiller à soupe
soup spoon

la serviette
napkin

la fourchette
fork

le couvert
place setting

la cuiller
spoon

le couteau
knife

la cuisine • kitchen

l'étagère
shelves

le revêtement
backsplash

le robinet
faucet

l'évier
sink

le tiroir
drawer

la hotte
extractor fan

la table de
cuisson
céramique
ceramic
range

le plan de
travail
countertop

le four
oven

le placard
cabinet

les appareils ménagers • appliances

le micro-ondes
microwave oven

le bol du mixeur
mixing bowl

la lame
blade

le couvercle
lid

la bouilloire
électrique
electric kettle

le grille-pain
toaster

le robot ménager
food processor

le mixeur
blender

le lave-vaisselle
dishwasher

le freezer
ice maker

le
congélateur
freezer

la clayette
shelf

le bac à
légumes
crisper

le réfrigérateur | refrigerator

vocabulaire • vocabulary

l'égouttoir draining board	**congeler** freeze (v)
le brûleur burner	**décongeler** defrost (v)
la table de cuisson stovetop	**cuire à la vapeur** steam (v)
la poubelle garbage can	**faire sauter** sauté (v)

la cuisine • cooking

éplucher
peel (v)

couper
slice (v)

râper
grate (v)

verser
pour (v)

mélanger
mix (v)

battre
whisk (v)

bouillir
boil (v)

frire
fry (v)

étaler au rouleau
roll (v)

remuer
stir (v)

mijoter
simmer (v)

pocher
poach (v)

cuire au four
bake (v)

rôtir
roast (v)

griller
broil (v)

les ustensiles de cuisine • kitchenware

le couteau à pain
bread knife

la planche à hacher
cutting board

le couteau de cuisine
kitchen knife

le fendoir
cleaver

l'aiguisoir
knife sharpener

l'attendrisseur
meat tenderizer

la broche
skewer

le pilon
pestle

l'épluche-légume
vegetable peeler

le vide-pomme
apple corer

la râpe
grater

le mortier
mortar

le presse-purée
potato masher

l'ouvre-boîte
can opener

l'ouvre-bouteille
bottle opener

le presse-ail
garlic press

la cuiller à servir
serving spoon

la pelle à poisson
slotted spatula

la passoire
colander

la spatule
spatula

la cuiller en bois
wooden spoon

l'écumoire
slotted spoon

la louche
ladle

la fourchette à découper
carving fork

la cuiller à glace
ice-cream scoop

le fouet
whisk

la passoire
sieve

le couvercle
lid

anti-adhérent
nonstick

la poêle
frying pan

la casserole
saucepan

le gril
grill pan

le wok
wok

le fait-tout
earthenware dish

en verre
glass

allant au four
ovenproof

le grand bol
mixing bowl

le moule à soufflé
soufflé dish

le plat à gratin
gratin dish

le ramequin
ramekin

la cocotte
casserole dish

la pâtisserie • baking cakes

la balance
scale

le verre mesureur
measuring cup

le moule à gâteaux
cake pan

la tourtière
pie pan

le moule à tarte
quiche pan

le pinceau à pâtisserie
pastry brush

le rouleau à pâtisserie
rolling pin

la poche à douille
piping bag

le moule à muffins
muffin pan

la plaque à gâteaux
baking sheet

la grille de refroidissement
cooling rack

le gant isolant
oven mitt

le tablier
apron

la chambre • bedroom

l'armoire
wardrobe

la lampe de chevet
bedside lamp

la tête de lit
headboard

la table de nuit
nightstand

la commode
chest of drawers

le tiroir
drawer

le lit
bed

le matelas
mattress

le couvre-lit
bedspread

l'oreiller
pillow

la bouillotte
hot-water bottle

le radio-réveil
clock radio

le réveil
alarm clock

la boîte de kleenex
box of tissues

le cintre
coathanger

le linge de lit • bed linen

la taie d'oreiller
pillowcase

le miroir
mirror

le drap
sheet

la frange de lit
dust ruffle

la coiffeuse
dressing
table

la couette
comforter

l'édredon
quilt

la
couverture
blanket

le sol
floor

---

vocabulaire • vocabulary

le lit simple twin bed	**le pied de lit** footboard	**l'insomnie** insomnia	**se réveiller** wake up (v)	**mettre le réveil** set the alarm (v)
le grand lit full bed	**le ressort** spring	**se coucher** go to bed (v)	**se lever** get up (v)	**ronfler** snore (v)
la couverture chauffante electric blanket	**le tapis** carpet	**s'endormir** go to sleep (v)	**faire le lit** make the bed (v)	**l'armoire encastrée** closet

la salle de bain • bathroom

le porte-
serviettes
towel bar

la porte de
douche
shower door

le robinet
d'eau froide
cold faucet

le robinet
d'eau chaude
hot faucet

le pommeau de
douche
shower head

le lavabo
sink

la douche
shower

la bonde
plug

le tuyau
d'écoulement
drain

le siège des
toilettes
toilet seat

la baignoire
bathtub

les toilettes
toilet

la brosse
toilet brush

le bidet | bidet

vocabulaire • vocabulary

l'armoire à pharmacie
medicine cabinet

le tapis de bain
bath mat

le rouleau de papier
hygiénique
toilet paper

le rideau de
douche
shower curtain

prendre une douche
take a shower (v)

prendre un bain
take a bath (v)

l'hygiène dentaire • dental hygiene

la brosse à dents
toothbrush

le fil
dentaire
dental floss

le dentifrice
toothpaste

l'eau dentifrice
mouthwash

l'éponge
sponge

la pierre ponce
pumice stone

la brosse pour le dos
back brush

le déodorant
deodorant

le porte-savon
soap dish

le gel douche
shower gel

le savon
soap

la crème pour le visage
moisturizer

le bain moussant
bubble bath

la serviette
hand towel

la serviette
de bain
bath towel

les serviettes
towels

la lotion pour le corps
body lotion

le talc
talcum powder

le peignoir
bathrobe

le rasage • shaving

le rasoir
électrique
electric razor

la lame de
rasoir
razor blade

la mousse à raser
shaving foam

le rasoir jetable
disposable razor

l'after-shave
aftershave

la chambre d'enfants • baby's room

les soins de bébé • baby care

la crème pour
l'érythème
diaper rash cream

la lingette
wet wipe

l'éponge
sponge

la baignoire en plastique
baby bath

le pot
potty

le matelas à langer
changing mat

le coucher • sleeping

le drap
sheet

la couverture
blanket

le mobile
mobile

les barreaux
bars

la couverture laineuse
fleece

la literie
bedding

le protège-barreaux
bumper

le matelas
mattress

le lit d'enfant | crib

le hochet
rattle

le moïse
bassinet

le jeu • playing

la poupée
doll

le jouet en peluche
soft toy

la maison de poupée
dollhouse

la maison pliante
playhouse

l'ours en peluche
teddy bear

le jouet
toy

la balle
ball

le panier à jouets
toy basket

le parc
playpen

la sécurité • safety

la serrure de sécurité
child lock

le moniteur
baby monitor

la barrière d'escalier
stair gate

le manger • eating

la chaise haute
high chair

la tétine
nipple

la tasse
drinking cup

le biberon
bottle

la sortie • going out

la capote
hood

la poussette
stroller

le landau
baby carriage

la couche
diaper

le couffin
carrier

le sac
diaper bag

le porte-bébé
baby sling

la buanderie • utility room

le linge • laundry

le linge propre
clean clothes

le linge sale
dirty laundry

le panier à linge
laundry basket

le lave-linge
washing machine

le lave-linge séchant
washer-dryer

le sèche-linge
tumble-dryer

le panier à linge
linen basket

la corde à linge
clothesline

le fer à repasser
iron

la pince à linge
clothespin

sécher
dry (v)

la planche à repasser | ironing board

---

vocabulaire • vocabulary

charger load (v)	**essorer** spin (v)	**repasser** iron (v)	**Comment fonctionne le lave-linge?** How do I operate the washing machine?
rincer rinse (v)	**l'essoreuse** spin-dryer	**l'assouplisseur** fabric softener	**Quel est le programme pour les couleurs/le blanc?** What is the setting for colors/whites?

l'équipement d'entretien • cleaning equipment

le tuyau flexible
hose

la balayette
brush

la pelle
dustpan

l'eau de Javel
bleach

le seau
pail

la poudre
laundry
powder

le liquide
liquid

le chiffon
duster

l'aspirateur
vacuum cleaner

le balai laveur
mop

le détergent
detergent

la cire
polish

les activités • activities

nettoyer
clean (v)

laver
wash (v)

essuyer
wipe (v)

laver à la brosse
scrub (v)

racler
scrape (v)

le balai
broom

balayer
sweep (v)

épousseter
dust (v)

cirer
polish (v)

l'atelier • workshop

le mandrin
chuck

la mèche
drill bit

la pile
battery pack

la scie sauteuse
jigsaw

la perceuse rechargeable
cordless drill

la perceuse électrique
electric drill

le pistolet à colle
glue gun

le serre-joint
clamp

la lame
blade

l'étau
vise

la ponceuse
sander

la scie circulaire
circular saw

l'établi
workbench

la colle à bois
wood glue

le porte-outils
tool rack

la guimbarde
router

le vilebrequin
bit brace

les copeaux
wood shavings

la rallonge
extension cord

les techniques • techniques

découper
cut (v)

scier
saw (v)

percer
drill (v)

marteler
hammer (v)

la soudure
solder

raboter
plane (v)

tourner
turn (v)

sculpter
carve (v)

souder
solder (v)

les matériaux • materials

le médium
MDF

le bois dur
hardwood

le fil de fer
wire

le contreplaqué
plywood

le câble
cable

l'aggloméré
chipboard

le vernis
varnish

l'inox
stainless steel

l'isorel
hardboard

la couleur
pour bois
wood stain

galvanisé
galvanized

le bois
tendre
softwood

le bois | wood

le métal | metal

la boîte à outils • toolbox

la clef
wrench

la clef à molette
adjustable wrench

le marteau
hammer

la pince plate
needle-nose pliers

la clef à pipe
socket wrench

les embouts
de tournevis
screwdriver
bits

le niveau
level

le joint
washer

le tournevis
screwdriver

l'écrou
nut

le mètre
tape measure

le couteau
utility knife

la pince universelle
bull-nose pliers

la douille
socket

la clef
Allen wrench

les forets • drill bits

le foret à métaux
metal bit

le foret à bois plat
flat wood bit

l'alésoir
reamer

le tournevis cruciforme
Phillips screwdriver

la tête
head

le foret de
sécurité
security bit

le clou
nail

les forets
à bois
carpentry bits

le foret de
maçonnerie
masonry bit

la vis
screw

la pince à dénuder
wire strippers

la pince coupante
wire cutters

le fer à souder
soldering iron

le ruban
isolant
insulating
tape

la soudure
solder

le scalpel
craft knife

la scie à
chantourner
fretsaw

la scie à dosseret | tenon saw

les lunettes de
sécurité
safety goggles

le rabot
plane

la scie égoïne
handsaw

la boîte à onglets
miter block

la scie à métaux
hacksaw

la perceuse
manuelle
hand drill

la paille de fer
steel wool

la clef serre-tube
wrench

le papier de verre
sandpaper

le burin
chisel

la ventouse
plunger

la lime
file

la pierre à
aiguiser
whetstone

le coupe-tube | pipe cutter

la décoration • decorating

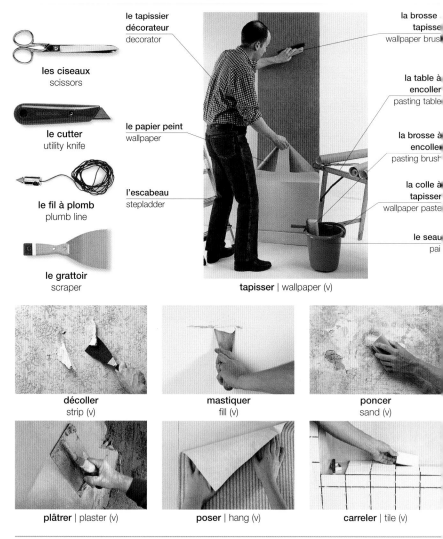

les ciseaux
scissors

le cutter
utility knife

le fil à plomb
plumb line

le grattoir
scraper

le tapissier
décorateur
decorator

le papier peint
wallpaper

l'escabeau
stepladder

la brosse à
tapisser
wallpaper brush

la table à
encoller
pasting table

la brosse à
encoller
pasting brush

la colle à
tapisser
wallpaper paste

le seau
pail

tapisser | wallpaper (v)

décoller | strip (v)

mastiquer | fill (v)

poncer | sand (v)

plâtrer | plaster (v)

poser | hang (v)

carreler | tile (v)

le rouleau
roller

le bac à peinture
paint tray

la peinture
paint

la brosse
brush

le pot de
peinture
paint can

l'éponge
sponge

le papier
cache
masking tape

le papier de
verre
sandpaper

le bleu
overalls

la térébenthine
turpentine

la couverture de
protection
dust sheet

le mastic
filler

le white-spirit
mineral spirits

peindre
paint (v)

---

vocabulaire • vocabulary

le plâtre plaster	**brillant** gloss	**le papier gaufré** embossed paper	**la couche de fond** undercoat	**l'enduit** sealant
le vernis varnish	**mat** mat	**le papier d'apprêt** lining paper	**la dernière couche** topcoat	**le solvant** solvent
la peinture mate latex paint	**le pochoir** stencil	**l'apprêt** primer	**l'agent de conservation** preservative	**le mastic** grout

---

le jardin • garden

les styles de jardin • garden styles

les ornements de jardin •
garden features

le patio
patio garden

le jardin sur le toit
roof garden

le panier suspendu
hanging basket

le jardin à la française | formal garden

la rocaille
rock garden

le treillis
trellis

le jardin paysan
cottage garden

le jardin d'herbes aromatiques
herb garden

la cour
courtyard

le jardin d'eau
water garden

la pergola
pergola

le sol • soil

le pavé
paving

l'allée
path

le tas de
compost
compost pile

le portail
gate

le parterre
flowerbed

la cabane
shed

la serre
greenhouse

la pelouse
lawn

la clôture
fence

le bassin
pond

la haie
hedge

l'arceau
arch

le potager
vegetable
garden

la bordure de plantes
herbacées
herbaceous border

les planches
decking

la fontaine | fountain

la terre
topsoil

le sable
sand

la chaux
chalk

la vase
silt

l'argile
clay

les plantes de jardin • garden plants

les genres de plantes • types of plants

annuel
annual

bisannuel
biennial

vivace
perennial

le bulbe
bulb

la fougère
fern

le jonc
rush

le bambou
bamboo

les mauvaises herbes
weeds

l'herbe
herb

la plante aquatique
water plant

l'arbre
tree

le palmier
palm

le conifère
conifer

à feuilles persistantes
evergreen

à feuilles caduques
deciduous

la topiaire
topiary

la plante alpestre
alpine

la plante grasse
succulent

le cactus
cactus

la plante en pot
potted plant

la plante d'ombre
shade plant

la plante
grimpante
climber

l'arbuste à
fleurs
flowering shrub

la couverture
du sol
ground cover

la plante rampante
creeper

ornemental
ornamental

l'herbe
grass

les outils de jardin • garden tools

le balai à gazon
lawn rake

le terreau
compost

les graines
seeds

la cendre d'os
bone meal

le gravier
gravel

la bêche
spade

la fourche
fork

la grande cisaille
long-handled shears

le râteau
rake

la houe
hoe

le sac à herbe
grass bag

le moteur
motor

le bras
handle

le panier de jardinier
trug

l'écran de
protection
shield

le support
stand

la tondeuse
trimmer

la tondeuse
lawnmower

la brouette
wheelbarrow

la petite fourche
hand fork

le sécateur
pruners

les gants de jardinage
gardening gloves

le déplantoir
trowel

la lame
blade

le germoir
seed tray

la ficelle
twine

les étiquettes
labels

les attaches
twist ties

les anneaux
ring ties

les cannes
canes

la cisaille
shears

le tamis
sieve

la scie à main
hand saw

le pesticide
pesticide

le pot à fleurs
plant pot

les bottes
rubber boots

l'arrosage • watering

le vaporisateur
spray bottle

l'arroseur
sprinkler

le jet
nozzle

l'arrosoir
watering can

le tuyau d'arrosage
hose

la pomme
spray

le dévidoir de tuyau | hose reel

le jardinage • gardening

la pelouse
lawn

la haie
hedge

le parterre
flowerbed

la tondeuse
lawnmower

le tuteur
stake

tondre | mow (v)

gazonner
sod (v)

piquer
spike (v)

ratisser
rake (v)

tailler
trim (v)

bêcher
dig (v)

semer
sow (v)

fumer en surface
top-dress (v)

arroser
water (v)

la canne
cane

palisser
train (v)

enlever les fleurs fanées
deadhead (v)

asperger
spray (v)

greffer
graft (v)

la coupe
cutting

propager
propagate (v)

élaguer
prune (v)

mettre un tuteur
stake (v)

transplanter
transplant (v)

désherber
weed (v)

pailler
mulch (v)

récolter
harvest (v)

vocabulaire • vocabulary

cultiver cultivate (v)	**dessiner** landscape (v)	**fertiliser** fertilize (v)	**tamiser** sift (v)	**biologique** organic	**le semis** seedling	**le sous-sol** subsoil
soigner tend (v)	**mettre en pot** pot (v)	**cueillir** pick (v)	**retourner** aerate (v)	**le drainage** drainage	**l'engrais** fertilizer	**l'herbicide** weedkiller

les services
services

les services d'urgence • emergency services

l'ambulance • ambulance

l'ambulance
ambulance

le brancard
stretcher

l'infirmier du SAMU
paramedic

la police • police

le badge
badge

l'uniforme
uniform

la sirène
siren

les feux
lights

la voiture de police
police car

le poste de police
police station

la matraque
nightstick

le pistolet
gun

les menottes
handcuffs

le policier
police officer

vocabulaire • vocabulary

l'inspecteur inspector	le suspect suspect	la plainte complaint	l'arrestation arrest
le crime crime	l'agression assault	l'enquête investigation	la cellule cell
l'officier de police detective	les empreintes fingerprint	le cambriolage burglary	l'accusation charge

les pompiers • fire department

la fumée
smoke

la casque
helmet

le tuyau
hose

les sapeurs-pompiers
firefighters

la nacelle
basket

le jet d'eau
water jet

la flèche
boom

l'échelle
ladder

la cabine
cab

l'incendie | fire

le poste d'incendie
fire station

l'escalier de secours
fire escape

la voiture de pompiers
fire engine

le détecteur de
fumée
smoke alarm

l'avertisseur
d'incendie
fire alarm

la hache
ax

l'extincteur
fire extinguisher

la borne
d'incendie
hydrant

| La police/les pompiers/une ambulance, s'il vous plaît. I need the police/fire department/ambulance. | Il y a un incendie à… There's a fire at… | Il y a eu un accident. There's been an accident. | Appelez la police! Call the police! |

la banque • bank

le client
customer

le guichet
window

le caissier
teller

les dépliants
brochures

le comptoir
counter

les fiches de
versement
deposit slips

la carte bancaire
debit card

le talon
stub

le numéro de
compte
account number

la signature
signature

le montant
amount

le directeur
d'agence
bank manager

la carte de crédit
credit card

le carnet de chèques
checkbook

le chèque
check

vocabulaire • vocabulary

l'épargne savings	l'hypothèque mortgage	le paiement payment	verser deposit (v)	le compte courant checking account
l'impôt tax	le découvert overdraft	le prélèvement automatic payment	les frais bancaires bank charge	le compte d'épargne savings account
le prêt loan	le taux d'intérêt interest rate	la fiche de retrait withdrawal slip	le virement bancaire electronic transfer	le code secret PIN

la pièce
coin

le billet
bill

l'écran
screen

le clavier
keypad

la fente
card slot

l'argent
money

le distributeur
ATM

les devises étrangères • foreign currency

le traveller
traveler's check

le bureau de change
bureau de change

le taux de change
exchange rate

la finance • finance

le prix des actions
share price

l'agent de la bourse
stockbroker

la conseillère financière
financial advisor

la bourse | stock exchange

vocabulaire • vocabulary

encaisser cash (v)	les actions shares
la valeur denomination	les dividendes dividends
la commission commission	le comptable accountant
l'investissement investment	le portefeuille portfolio
les titres stocks	l'action equity

Est-ce que je peux changer ça, s'il vous plaît?
Can I change this, please?

Quel est le taux de change aujourd'hui?
What's today's exchange rate?

les communications • communications

le postier
postal worker

le guichet
window

la balance
scale

le guichet
counter

la poste | post office

le tampon de la poste
postmark

le timbre
stamp

l'adresse
address

le code postal
ZIP code

l'enveloppe | envelope

le facteur
mail carrier

vocabulaire • vocabulary

la lettre letter	**l'expéditeur** return address	**la distribution** delivery	**fragile** fragile	**ne pas plier** do not bend (v)
par avion by airmail	**la signature** signature	**le mandat postal** money order	**le sac postal** mailbag	**dessus** this way up
l'envoi en recommandé registered mail	**la levée** pickup	**le tarif d'affranchissement** postage	**le télégramme** telegram	**le fax** fax

la boîte aux lettres
mailbox

la boîte aux lettres
letterslot

le colis
package

le service de messagerie
courier

le téléphone • telephone

le combiné
handset

le répondeur
answering machine

la base
base station

le téléphone sans fil
cordless phone

le visiophone
video phone

la cabine téléphonique
telephone booth

le clavier
keypad

le smartphone
smartphone

le portable
cell phone

le combiné
receiver

les pièces rendues
coin return

le téléphone public
payphone

---

vocabulaire • vocabulary

les renseignements directory assistance	**le SMS** text (SMS)	**coupé** disconnected	**Pouvez-vous me donner le numéro pour…?** Can you give me the number for…?
le P.C.V. collect call	**le message vocal** voice message	**l'appli** app	**Quel est l'indicatif pour…?** What is the area code for…?
composer dial (v)	**le téléphoniste** operator	**le mot de passe** passcode	**Envoie-moi un SMS!** Text me!
répondre answer (v)	**occupé** busy		

---

l'hôtel • hotel
le hall • lobby

le client
guest

la clef de la chambre
room key

les messages
messages

le casier
pigeonhole

la réceptionniste
receptionist

le registre
register

le comptoir
counter

la réception | reception

les bagages
luggage

le diable
cart

le porteur
porter

l'ascenseur
elevator

le numéro de chambre
room number

les chambres • rooms

la chambre simple
single room

la chambre double
double room

la chambre à deux lits
twin room

la salle de bain privée
private bathroom

les services • services

le plateau à petit déjeuner
breakfast tray

le service de ménage
maid service

le service de blanchisserie
laundry service

le service d'étage | room service

le minibar
mini bar

le restaurant
restaurant

la salle de sport
gym

la piscine
swimming pool

---

vocabulaire • vocabulary

la chambre avec le petit déjeuner
bed and breakfast

Avez-vous une chambre de libre?
Do you have any vacancies?

Je voudrais une chambre pour trois nuits.
I'd like a room for three nights.

la pension complète
full board

J'ai une réservation.
I have a reservation.

C'est combien par nuit?
What is the charge per night?

la demi-pension
half-board

Je voudrais une chambre simple.
I'd like a single room.

Quand est-ce que je dois quitter la chambre?
When do I have to check out?

---

les courses
shopping

le centre commercial • shopping center

l'atrium
atrium

le deuxième
étage
third floor

l'enseigne
sign

le premier
étage
second
floor

l'escalier
mécanique
escalator

l'ascenseur
elevator

le rez-de-
chaussée
ground floor

le client
customer

vocabulaire • vocabulary

le rayon enfants
children's department

le guide
store directory

les cabines d'essayage
changing rooms

C'est combien?
How much is this?

le rayon bagages
luggage department

le vendeur
sales clerk

les soins de bébés
baby changing facilities

**Est-ce que je peux
changer ça?**
May I exchange this?

le rayon chaussures
shoe department

**le service
après-vente**
customer services

les toilettes
restrooms

le grand magasin • department store

les vêtements pour
hommes
menswear

les vêtement pour
femmes
women's clothing

la lingerie
lingerie

la parfumerie
perfume

la beauté
beauty

le linge de maison
linen

l'ameublement
home furnishings

la mercerie
notions

la vaisselle
kitchenware

la porcelaine
china

l'électroménager
electrical goods

l'éclairage
lighting

les articles de sport
sports

les jouets
toys

la papeterie
stationery

l'alimentation
food

le supermarché • supermarket

le tapis roulant
conveyer belt

le caissier
checker

les promotions
specials

l'allée
aisle

l'étagère
shelf

la caisse | checkout

le client
customer

la caisse
cash
register

**la sac à
provisions**
shopping bag

les provisions
groceries

l'anse
handle

780863 185779
le code barres
bar code

le caddie
cart

le panier
basket

le lecteur optique
scanner

la boulangerie
bakery

la crémerie
dairy

les céréales
cereals

les conserves
canned food

la confiserie
candy

les légumes
vegetables

les fruits
fruit

la viande et la volaille
meat and poultry

le poisson
fish

la charcuterie
deli

les produits surgelés
frozen food

les plats cuisinés
convenience food

les boissons
drinks

les produits d'entretien
household products

les articles de toilette
toiletries

les articles pour bébés
baby products

l'électroménager
electrical goods

la nourriture pour animaux
pet food

les magazines | magazines

la pharmacie • drugstore

les soins dentaires
dental care

l'hygiène féminine
feminine hygiene

les déodorants
deodorants

les vitamines
vitamins

l'officine
pharmacy

le pharmacien
pharmacist

le médicament pour la toux
cough medicine

l'herboristerie
herbal remedies

les soins de la peau
skin care

l'après-soleil
aftersun

l'écran solaire
sunscreen

l'écran total
sunblock

le produit anti-insecte
insect repellent

la lingette humide
wet wipe

le kleenex
tissue

la serviette hygiénique
sanitary napkin

le tampon
tampon

le protège-slip
panty liner

la cuiller pour
mesurer
measuring spoon

le mode d'emploi
instructions

la gélule
capsule

la pilule
pill

le sirop
syrup

l'inhalateur
inhaler

la crème
cream

la pommade
ointment

le gel
gel

le suppositoire
suppository

le compte-
gouttes
dropper

l'aiguille
needle

les gouttes
drops

la seringue
syringe

le spray
spray

la poudre
powder

vocabulaire • vocabulary

le fer iron	**l'insuline** insulin	**jetable** disposable	**le médicament** medicine	**l'analgésique** painkiller
le calcium calcium	**les effets secondaires** side effects	**soluble** soluble	**le laxatif** laxative	**le sédatif** sedative
le magnésium magnesium	**la date d'expiration** expiration date	**la posologie** dosage	**la diarrhée** diarrhea	**le somnifère** sleeping pill
le médicament multivitamine multivitamins	**les cachets antinaupathiques** travel sickness pills	**la médication** medication	**la pastille pour la gorge** cough drop	**l'anti-inflammatoire** anti-inflammatory

français • english

le fleuriste • florist

les fleurs
flowers

le lis
lily

l'acacia
acacia

l'œillet
carnation

la plante en pot
potted plant

le glaïeul
gladiolus

l'iris
iris

la marguerite
daisy

le
chrysanthème
chrysanthemum

la gypsophile
gypsophila

| la giroflée | le gerbera | le feuillage | la rose | le freesia |
| stocks | gerbera | foliage | rose | freesia |

le vase
vase

l'orchidée
orchid

la pivoine
peony

la botte
bunch

la tige
stem

la jonquille
daffodil

le bourgeon
bud

l'emballage
wrapping

la tulipe | tulip

les compositions florales • arrangements

le ruban
ribbon

le bouquet
bouquet

les fleurs séchées
dried flowers

le pot-pourri | potpourri

la couronne | wreath

la guirlande
de fleurs
garland

Je peux y attacher un message? Can I attach a message?	**Elles tiennent combien de temps?** How long will these last?
Est-ce qu'elles sentent bon? Are they fragrant?	**Pouvez-vous les envoyer à...?** Can you send them to....?
Pouvez-vous les emballer? Can I have them wrapped?	**Je voudrais un bouquet de..., SVP.** Can I have a bunch of..., please.

le marchand de journaux • newsstand

les cigarettes
cigarettes

le paquet de cigarettes
pack of cigarettes

les timbres
stamps

la carte postale
postcard

la bande dessinée
comic book

le magazine
magazine

le journal
newspaper

fumer • smoking

le tuyau
stem

le fourneau
bowl

le tabac
tobacco

le briquet
lighter

la pipe
pipe

le cigare
cigar

le confiseur • confectionery

la boîte de chocolats
box of chocolates

la friandise
snack bar

les chips
chips

la confiserie | candy store

la confiserie • confectionery

le chocolat
chocolate

la tablette de chocolat
chocolate bar

les bonbons
candies

la sucette
lollipop

le caramel
toffee

le nougat
nougat

la guimauve
marshmallow

le bonbon à la menthe
mint

le chewing-gum
chewing gum

la dragée à la gelée
jellybean

le bonbon au fruit
gumdrop

le réglisse
licorice

les autres magasins • other stores

la boulangerie
bread shop

la pâtisserie
bakery

la boucherie
butcher shop

la poissonnerie
fish-seller

le marchand de légumes
produce stand

l'épicerie
grocery store

le magasin de chaussures
shoe store

la quincaillerie
hardware store

le magasin d'antiquités
antique store

la boutique de cadeaux
gift shop

l'agence de voyage
travel agent

la bijouterie
jewelry store

la librairie
bookstore

le magasin de disques
record store

le magasin de vins et spiritueux
liquor store

l'animalerie
pet store

le magasin de meubles
furniture store

la boutique
boutique

vocabulaire • vocabulary

l'agent immobilier realtor	le magasin d'appareils photos camera store
la pépinière garden center	le magasin bio health food store
le pressing dry-cleaner	la boutique d'art art store
la laverie automatique laundromat	le marchand d'occasion second-hand store

le tailleur
tailor shop

le salon de coiffure
beauty salon

le marché | market

la nourriture
food

la viande • meat

l'agneau
lamb

le boucher
butcher

l'allonge
meat hook

la balance
scale

le fusil
knife sharpener

le bacon
bacon

les saucisses
sausages

le foie
liver

vocabulaire • vocabulary

le porc pork	**la venaison** venison	**les abats** offal	**de ferme** free range	**la viande rouge** red meat
le bœuf beef	**le lapin** rabbit	**salé** cured	**naturel** organic	**la viande maigre** lean meat
le veau veal	**la langue de bœuf** tongue	**fumé** smoked	**la viande blanche** white meat	**la viande cuite** cooked meat

les morceaux de viande • cuts

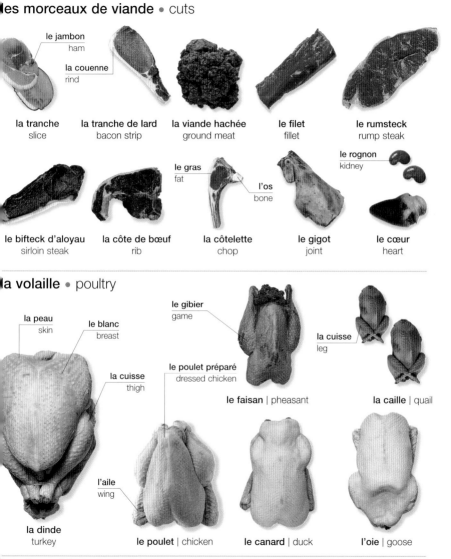

le jambon
ham

la couenne
rind

la tranche
slice

la tranche de lard
bacon strip

la viande hachée
ground meat

le filet
fillet

le rumsteck
rump steak

le gras
fat

l'os
bone

le rognon
kidney

le bifteck d'aloyau
sirloin steak

la côte de bœuf
rib

la côtelette
chop

le gigot
joint

le cœur
heart

la volaille • poultry

la peau
skin

le blanc
breast

le gibier
game

la cuisse
leg

le poulet préparé
dressed chicken

la cuisse
thigh

le faisan | pheasant

la caille | quail

l'aile
wing

la dinde
turkey

le poulet | chicken

le canard | duck

l'oie | goose

le poisson • fish

les crevettes
décortiquées
peeled shrimp

le rouget barbet
red mullet

les filets de
flétan
halibut fillets

la truite arc-en-ciel
rainbow trout

la glace
ice

les ailes de raie
skate wings

la poissonnerie
fish counter

la lotte
monkfish

le maquereau
mackerel

la truite
trout

l'espadon
swordfish

la sole
Dover sole

la limande-sole
lemon sole

l'aiglefin
haddock

la sardine
sardine

la raie
skate

le merlan
whiting

le bar
sea bass

le saumon | salmon

la morue
cod

la daurade
sea bream

le thon
tuna

les fruits de mer • seafood

la coquille Saint-Jacques
scallop

le homard
lobster

le crabe
crab

la crevette
jumbo
shrimp

la moule
mussel

l'écrevisse
crayfish

le couteau
razorshell clam

l'huître
oyster

la coque
cockle

la pieuvre
octopus

la seiche
cuttlefish

le calamar
squid

le clam
clam

---

vocabulaire • vocabulary

surgelé	préparé	fumé	écaillé	le filet	la longe	la queue	l'arête	l'écaille
frozen	cleaned	smoked	descaled	fillet	loin	tail	bone	scale

frais	salé	sans peau	sans arêtes	en filets	la tranche	Pouvez-vous le préparer pour moi?
fresh	salted	skinned	boned	filleted	steak	Will you clean it for me?

---

les légumes 1 • vegetables 1

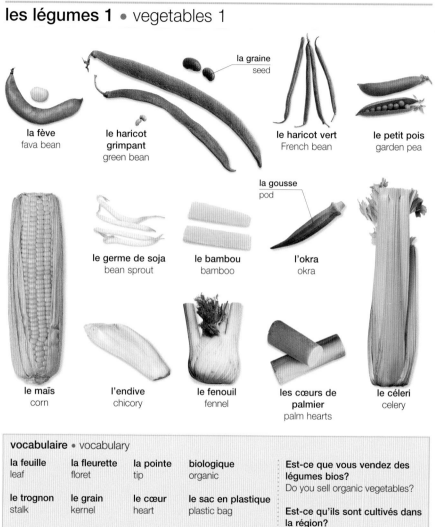

la graine
seed

la fève
fava bean

le haricot grimpant
green bean

le haricot vert
French bean

le petit pois
garden pea

le germe de soja
bean sprout

le bambou
bamboo

la gousse
pod

l'okra
okra

le maïs
corn

l'endive
chicory

le fenouil
fennel

les cœurs de palmier
palm hearts

le céleri
celery

vocabulaire • vocabulary

la feuille leaf	**la fleurette** floret	**la pointe** tip	**biologique** organic	**Est-ce que vous vendez des légumes bios?** Do you sell organic vegetables?
le trognon stalk	**le grain** kernel	**le cœur** heart	**le sac en plastique** plastic bag	**Est-ce qu'ils sont cultivés dans la région?** Are these grown locally?

la roquette
arugula

le cresson
watercress

le radicchio
radicchio

le chou de Bruxelles
Brussels sprout

la bette
Swiss chard

le chou frisé
kale

l'oseille
sorrel

la chicorée
endive

le pissenlit
dandelion

les épinards
spinach

le chou-rave
kohlrabi

le chou chinois
pak-choi

la laitue
lettuce

le brocoli
broccoli

le chou
cabbage

le chou précoce
spring greens

les légumes 2 • vegetables 2

le navet
turnip

l'artichaut
artichoke

le radis
radish

le chou-fleur
cauliflower

l'asperge
asparagus

la pomme de terre
potato

la courge
marrow
squash

l'oignon
onion

le poivron
pepper

le piment
chili pepper

le maïs
sweetcorn

---

vocabulaire • vocabulary

la tomate cerise cherry tomato	**le céleri** celeriac	**surgelé** frozen	**amer** bitter	**Puis-je avoir un kilo de pommes de terre s'il vous plaît?** Can I have one kilo of potatoes, please?
la carotte carrot	**le taro** taro root	**cru** raw	**ferme** firm	
le fruit de l'arbre à pain breadfruit	**le manioc** cassava	**épicé** hot (spicy)	**la pulpa** flesh	**C'est combien le kilo?** What's the price per kilo?
la pomme de terre nouvelle new potato	**la châtaigne d'eau** water chestnut	**sucré** sweet	**la racine** root	**Ils s'appellent comment?** What are those called?

la patate douce
sweet potato

l'igname
yam

la betterave
beet

le rutabaga
rutabaga

le topinambour
Jerusalem
artichoke

le raifort
horseradish

le panais
parsnip

le gingembre
ginger

l'aubergine
eggplant

la tomate
tomato

la ciboule
green onion

le poireau
leek

l'échalote
shallot

l'ail
garlic

la gousse
clove

la truffe
truffle

le champignon
mushroom

le concombre
cucumber

la courgette
zucchini

**la courge
musquée**
butternut squash

la courge gland
acorn squash

la citrouille
pumpkin

le fruit 1 • fruit 1

les agrumes • citrus fruit

l'orange
orange

la clémentine
clementine

la peau blanche
pith

le tangelo
ugli fruit

le pamplemousse
grapefruit

le quartier
segment

la mandarine
tangerine

la satsuma
satsuma

le zeste
zest

le citron vert
lime

le citron
lemon

le kumquat
kumquat

les fruits à noyau • stone fruit

la pêche
peach

la nectarine
nectarine

l'abricot
apricot

la prune
plum

la cerise
cherry

la poire
pear

la pomme
apple

la corbeille de fruits | basket of fruit

les fruits rouges et les melons • berries and melons

la fraise
strawberry

la framboise
raspberry

le melon
melon

les raisins
grapes

la mûre
blackberry

la groseille
red currant

la canneberge
cranberry

le cassis
black currant

l'écorce
rind

le pépin
seed

la pulpe
flesh

la myrtille
blueberry

la groseille blanche
white currant

la pastèque
watermelon

la loganberry
loganberry

la groseille à maquereau
gooseberry

vocabulaire • vocabulary

la rhubarbe rhubarb	**aigre** sour	**croquant** crisp	**le jus** juice	**Est-ce qu'ils sont mûrs?** Are they ripe?
la fibra fiber	**frais** fresh	**pourri** rotten	**le trognon** core	**Je peux goûter?** Can I try one?
sucré sweet	**juteux** juicy	**la pulpe** pulp	**sans pépins** seedless	**Ils se gardent combien de temps?** How long will they keep?

les fruits 2 • fruit 2

la mangue
mango

l'ananas
pineapple

l'avocat
avocado

la papaye
papaya

la pêche
peach

le litchi
lychee

le kiwi
kiwifruit

le physalis
cape gooseberry

le pépin
seed

la peau
skin

le coing
quince

le fruit de la passion
passion fruit

la banane
banana

la goyave
guava

la grenade
pomegranate

le kaki
persimmon

le feijoa
feijoa

la figue de Barbarie
prickly pear

la carambole
starfruit

le tamarillo
tamarillo

les noix et les fruits secs • nuts and dried fruit

le pignon
pine nut

la pistache
pistachio

la noix de cajou
cashew

la cacahouète
peanut

la noisette
hazelnut

la noix du Brésil
Brazil nut

la noix pacane
pecan

l'amande
almond

la noix
walnut

le marron
chestnut

le macadamia
macadamia

la figue
fig

la datte
date

le pruneau
prune

la coquille
shell

le raisin de Smyrne
sultana raisin

le raisin sec
raisin

le raisin de Corinthe
currant

la chair
flesh

la noix de coco
coconut

vocabulaire • vocabulary

vert green	**dur** hard	**l'amande** kernel	**salé** salted	**grillé** roasted	**décortiqué** shelled	**le fruit confit** candied fruit
mûr ripe	**mou** soft	**séché** desiccated	**cru** raw	**de saison** seasonal	**complet** whole	**les fruits tropicaux** tropical fruit

les céréales et les légumes secs • grains and legumes

les céréales • grains

le blé	l'avoine	l'orge
wheat	oats	barley

le millet	le maïs	le quinoa
millet	corn	quinoa

vocabulaire • vocabulary

la graine seed	**parfumé** fragranced	**facile à cuisiner** easy-cook
la balle husk	**la céréale** cereal	**à grains longs** long-grain
le grain kernel	**complet** whole-grain	**à grains ronds** short-grain
sec dry	**laisser tremper** soak (v)	
frais fresh		

le riz • rice

le riz blanc	le riz complet
white rice	brown rice

le riz sauvage	le riz rond
wild rice	pudding rice

les céréales traitées • processed grains

le couscous	le blé écrasé
couscous	cracked wheat

la semoule	le son
semolina	bran

les haricots et les pois • beans and peas

les gros haricots blancs
butter beans

les haricots blancs
haricot beans

les haricots rouges
red kidney beans

les adzukis
aduki beans

les fèves
fava beans

les graines de soja
soybeans

les haricots à œil noir
black-eyed beans

les haricots pinto
pinto beans

les haricots mung
mung beans

les flageolets
flageolet beans

les lentilles
brown lentils

les lentilles rouges
red lentils

les petits pois
green peas

les pois chiches
garbanzos

les pois cassés
split peas

les graines • seeds

la graine de potiron
pumpkin seed

le grain de moutarde
mustard seed

la graine de carvi
caraway

la graine de sésame
sesame seed

la graine de tournesol
sunflower seed

les herbes et les épices • herbs and spices

les épices • spices

la vanille
vanilla

la noix de muscade
nutmeg

le macis
mace

le curcuma
turmeric

le cumin
cumin

le bouquet garni
bouquet garni

le poivre de la Jamaïque
allspice

le grain de poivre
peppercorn

le fenugrec
fenugreek

le piment
chili powder

en morceaux
whole

écrasé
crushed

le safran
saffron

la cardamome
cardamom

la poudre de curry
curry powder

en poudre
ground

le paprika
paprika

en flocons
flakes

l'ail
garlic

les herbes • herbs

les bâtons
sticks

la cannelle
cinnamon

la citronnelle
lemon grass

le clou de girofle
cloves

l'anis étoilé
star anise

le gingembre
ginger

le fenouil
fennel

les graines de
fenouil
fennel seeds

la ciboulette
chives

l'estragon
tarragon

l'origan
oregano

la menthe
mint

la marjolaine
marjoram

la coriandre
cilantro

la feuille de laurier
bay leaf

le thym
thyme

le basilic
basil

l'aneth
dill

le persil
parsley

la sauge
sage

le romarin
rosemary

les aliments en bouteilles • bottled foods

l'huile de noix
walnut oil

l'huile de pépins
de raisin
grapeseed oil

le bouchon
cork

l'huile de
tournesol
sunflower oil

l'huile
d'amande
almond oil

l'huile de
sésame
sesame oil

l'huile de noisette
hazelnut oil

l'huile d'olive
olive oil

les herbes
herbs

l'huile parfumée
flavored oil

les huiles
oils

les produits à tartiner • sweet spreads

le pot
jar

le gâteau de miel
honeycomb

le miel solide
candied honey

la pâte à tartiner
au citron
lemon curd

la confiture de
framboises
raspberry jam

la confiture
d'oranges
marmalade

le miel liquide
clear honey

le sirop
d'érable
maple syrup

les condiments • condiments and spreads

le vinaigre de
cidre
cider vinegar

le vinaigre
balsamique
balsamic vinegar

la bouteille
bottle

la mayonnaise
mayonnaise

le ketchup
ketchup

la moutarde
anglaise
English mustard

la moutarde
française
French mustard

le chutney
chutney

le vinaigre de malt
malt vinegar

le vinaigre de vin
wine vinegar

le vinaigre
vinegar

la sauce
sauce

la moutarde
en grains
whole-grain
mustard

le bocal scellé
sealed jar

le beurre de
cacahouètes
peanut butter

la pâte à tartiner
au chocolat
chocolate spread

les fruits en
bocaux
preserved fruit

vocabulaire • vocabulary

l'huile de maïs
corn oil

l'huile de colza
canola oil

l'huile
d'arachide
peanut oil

l'huile pressée
à froid
cold-pressed oil

l'huile végétale
vegetable oil

les produits laitiers • dairy products

le fromage • cheese

la croûte
rind

le fromage à pâte
pressée non cuite
semi-hard cheese

le fromage râpé
grated cheese

le fromage à pâte pressée cuite
hard cheese

le fromage à pâte
semi-molle
semi-soft cheese

le cottage
cottage
cheese

le fromage à
la crème
cream cheese

le bleu
blue cheese

le fromage à pâte molle
soft cheese

le fromage frais | fresh cheese

le lait • milk

le lait
entier
whole milk

le lait demi-écrémé
reduced-fat milk

le lait écrémé
skim milk

le carton de lait
milk carton

le lait de
chèvre
goat's milk

le lait condensé
condensed milk

le lait de vache | cow's milk

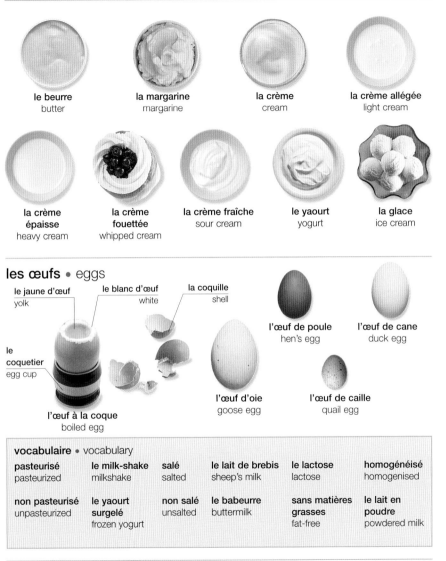

le beurre
butter

la margarine
margarine

la crème
cream

la crème allégée
light cream

la crème épaisse
heavy cream

la crème fouettée
whipped cream

la crème fraîche
sour cream

le yaourt
yogurt

la glace
ice cream

les œufs • eggs

le jaune d'œuf
yolk

le blanc d'œuf
white

la coquille
shell

l'œuf de poule
hen's egg

l'œuf de cane
duck egg

le coquetier
egg cup

l'œuf d'oie
goose egg

l'œuf de caille
quail egg

l'œuf à la coque
boiled egg

vocabulaire • vocabulary

pasteurisé pasteurized	**le milk-shake** milkshake	**salé** salted	**le lait de brebis** sheep's milk	**le lactose** lactose	**homogénéisé** homogenised
non pasteurisé unpasteurized	**le yaourt surgelé** frozen yogurt	**non salé** unsalted	**le babeurre** buttermilk	**sans matières grasses** fat-free	**le lait en poudre** powdered milk

les pains et la farine • breads and flours

le pain tranché
sliced bread

les graines de pavot
poppy seeds

le pain de seigle
rye bread

la baguette
baguette

la boulangerie | bread shop

faire du pain • making bread

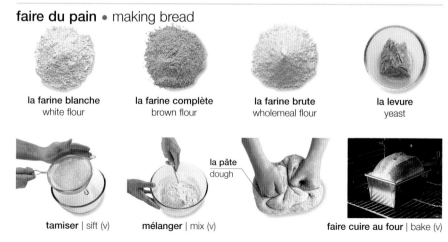

la farine blanche
white flour

la farine complète
brown flour

la farine brute
wholemeal flour

la levure
yeast

tamiser | sift (v)

mélanger | mix (v)

la pâte
dough

faire cuire au four | bake (v)

la croûte
crust

le pain
loaf

la tranche
slice

le pain blanc
white bread

le pain bis
brown bread

le pain de son
whole-wheat bread

le pain complet
multigrain bread

le pain de maïs
corn bread

le pain au bicarbonate de soude
soda bread

le pain au levain
sourdough bread

le pain plat
flatbread

le petit pain américain
bagel

le petit pain rond
bun

le petit pain
roll

le pain aux raisins secs
fruit bread

le pain aux graines
seeded bread

le naan
naan bread

le pita
pita bread

le biscuit scandinave
crispbread

vocabulaire • vocabulary

la farine traitée bread flour	**se lever** rise (v)	**lever** prove (v)	**la chapelure** breadcrumbs	**la machine à couper** slicer
la farine avec la levure self-rising flour	**la farine sans levure** all-purpose flour	**glacer** glaze (v)	**la flûte** flute	**le boulanger** baker

les gâteaux et les desserts • cakes and desserts

l'éclair
éclair

la pâte à choux
choux pastry

la pâte feuilletée
puff pastry

la crème
cream

la pâte de filo
phyllo pastry

la garniture
filling

enrobé de chocolat
chocolate-coated

le cake
fruitcake

le muffin
muffin

la tarte aux fruits
fruit tart

la madeleine
sponge cake

la meringue
meringue

les gâteaux | cakes

vocabulaire • vocabulary

la crème pâtissière crème patisserie	**le petit gâteau** sweet bun	**la pâte** pastry	**le riz au lait** rice pudding	**Est-ce que je peux avoir une tranche s'il vous plaît?** May I have a slice, please?
le gâteau au chocolat chocolate cake	**la crème anglaise** custard	**la tranche** slice	**la fête** celebration	

les pépites de
chocolat
chocolate chip

les **boudoirs**
lady fingers

le **florentine**
florentine

le **diplomate**
trifle

les **biscuits** | cookies

la **mousse**
mousse

le **sorbet**
sherbet

la **tarte à la crème**
cream pie

la **crème caramel**
crème caramel

les gâteaux de fête • celebration cakes

l'étage **supérieur**
top tier

le **ruban**
ribbon

l'étage
inférieur
bottom tier

le **glaçage**
frosting

la **pâte
d'amandes**
marzipan

la
décoration
decoration

les **bougies
d'anniversaire**
birthday candles

souffler
blow out (v)

le **gâteau de mariage** | wedding cake

le **gâteau d'anniversaire** | birthday cake

la charcuterie • delicatessen

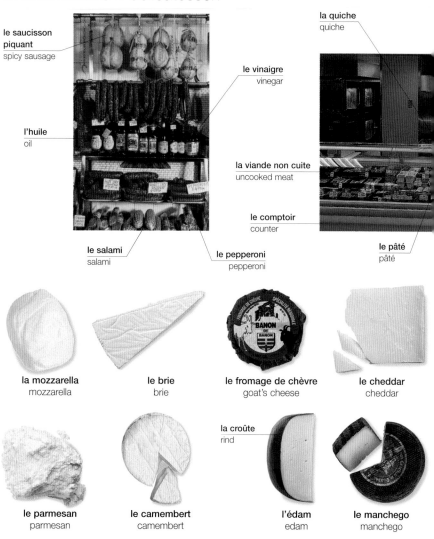

le saucisson piquant
spicy sausage

la quiche
quiche

le vinaigre
vinegar

l'huile
oil

la viande non cuite
uncooked meat

le comptoir
counter

le salami
salami

le pepperoni
pepperoni

le pâté
pâté

la mozzarella
mozzarella

le brie
brie

le fromage de chèvre
goat's cheese

le cheddar
cheddar

le parmesan
parmesan

le camembert
camembert

la croûte
rind

l'édam
edam

le manchego
manchego

les pâtés en croûte
meat pies

l'olive noire
black olive

le piment
chili
pepper

la sauce
sauce

le petit pain
bread roll

la viande cuite
cooked meat

l'olive verte
green olive

le jambon
ham

le comptoir sandwichs
sandwich counter

le poisson fumé
smoked fish

les câpres
capers

le chorizo
chorizo

le prosciutto
prosciutto

l'olive fourrée
stuffed olive

vocabulaire • vocabulary

à l'huile in oil	**mariné** marinated	**fumé** smoked
en saumure in brine	**salé** salted	**séché** cured

Prenez un numéro, s'il vous plaît.
Take a number, please.

**Est-ce que je peut goûter un peu de ça,
s'il vous plaît?**
Can I try some of that, please?

Je voudrais six tranches, s'il vous plaît.
May I have six slices of that, please?

les boissons • drinks

l'eau • water

les boissons chaudes • hot drinks

l'eau en bouteille
bottled water

l'eau du robinet
tap water

gazeux
sparkling

non gazeux
still

le sachet de thé
teabag

les feuilles de thé
loose tea

le thé
tea

les grains
beans

le café moulu
ground coffee

le café
coffee

le tonic
tonic water

l'eau minérale
mineral water

le soda
soda water

le chocolat chaud
hot chocolate

la boisson maltée
malted drink

les boissons non alcoolisées • soft drinks

la paille
straw

le jus de tomate
tomato juice

le jus de raisin
grape juice

la limonade
lemonade

l'orangeade
orangeade

le coca
cola

les boissons alcoolisées • alcoholic drinks

le gin
gin

la boîte
can

la bière
beer

le cidre
cider

la bière anglaise
bitter

la bière brune
stout

la vodka
vodka

le whisky
whiskey

le rhum
rum

le brandy
brandy

le porto
port

sec
dry

le sherry
sherry

le campari
campari

la liqueur
liqueur

la téquila
tequila

le champagne
champagne

rosé
rosé

blanc
white

rouge
red

le vin
wine

sortir manger
eating out

le café • café

le parasol
umbrella

le store
awning

le menu
menu

la terrasse de café
terrace café

le serveur
waiter

le percolateur
coffee machine

la table
table

la terrasse de café | sidewalk café

le snack | snack bar

le café • coffee

le crème
coffee with
milk

le noir
black coffee

le chocolat en
poudre
cocoa powder

la mousse
froth

le café filtre
filter coffee

l'expresso
espresso

le cappuccino
cappuccino

le café glacé
iced coffee

le thé • tea

la tisane
herbal tea

la camomille
chamomile tea

le thé vert
green tea

le thé au lait
tea with milk

le thé nature
plain tea

le thé au citron
tea with lemon

l'infusion de menthe
mint tea

le thé glacé
iced tea

les jus et milk-shakes • juices and milkshakes

le milk-shake au chocolat
chocolate milkshake

le milk-shake à la fraise
strawberry milkshake

le milk-shake au café
coffee milkshake

le jus d'orange
orange juice

le jus de pomme
apple juice

le jus d'ananas
pineapple juice

le jus de tomate
tomato juice

la nourriture • food

la boule
scoop

le pain bis
brown bread

le sandwich grillé
toasted sandwich

la salade
salad

la glace
ice cream

la pâtisserie
pastry

le bar • bar

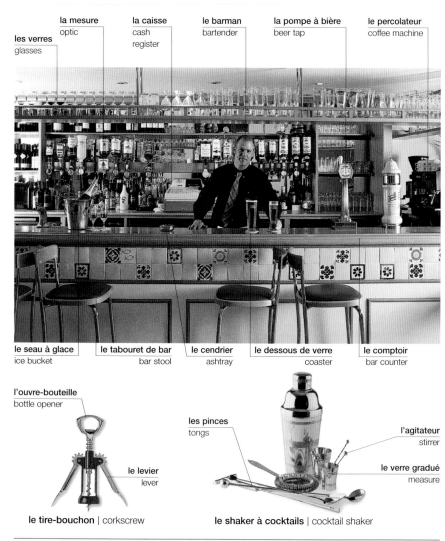

la mesure optic	**la caisse** cash register	**le barman** bartender	**la pompe à bière** beer tap	**le percolateur** coffee machine
les verres glasses					

le seau à glace
ice bucket

le tabouret de bar
bar stool

le cendrier
ashtray

le dessous de verre
coaster

le comptoir
bar counter

l'ouvre-bouteille
bottle opener

les pinces
tongs

l'agitateur
stirrer

le levier
lever

le verre gradué
measure

le tire-bouchon | corkscrew

le shaker à cocktails | cocktail shaker

le pichet
pitcher

le glaçon
ice cube

le gin tonic
gin and tonic

le scotch à l'eau
scotch and water

le rhum coca
rum and cola

la vodka à l'orange
screwdriver

le martini
martini

le cocktail
cocktail

le vin
wine

la bière | beer

double
double

simple
single

citron et glaçons
ice and lemon

un coup
shot

la mesure
measure

sans glaçons
without ice

avec des glaçons
with ice

les amuse-gueule • bar snacks

les noix
de cajou
cashews

les
cacahouètes
peanuts

les amandes
almonds

les chips | chips

les noix | nuts

les olives | olives

le restaurant • restaurant

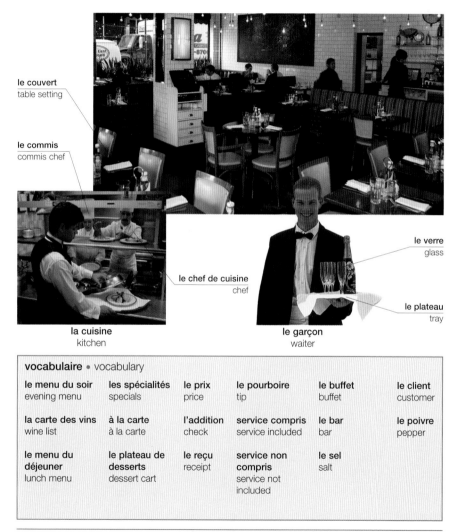

le couvert
table setting

le commis
commis chef

le chef de cuisine
chef

le verre
glass

le plateau
tray

la cuisine
kitchen

le garçon
waiter

---

vocabulaire • vocabulary

le menu du soir evening menu	**les spécialités** specials	**le prix** price	**le pourboire** tip	**le buffet** buffet	**le client** customer
la carte des vins wine list	**à la carte** à la carte	**l'addition** check	**service compris** service included	**le bar** bar	**le poivre** pepper
le menu du déjeuner lunch menu	**le plateau de desserts** dessert cart	**le reçu** receipt	**service non compris** service not included	**le sel** salt	

la carte
menu

le menu d'enfant
children's meal

commander
order (v)

payer
pay (v)

les plats • courses

l'apéritif
apéritif

l'entrée
appetizer

la soupe
soup

le plat principal
entrée

l'accompagnement
side order

le dessert | dessert

le café | coffee

Une table pour deux, s'il vous plaît.
A table for two, please.

La carte/la carte des vins, s'il vous plaît.
Can I see the menu/wine list, please?

Avez-vous un menu à prix fixe?
Is there a fixed-price menu?

Avez vous des plats végétariens?
Do you have any vegetarian dishes?

L'addition/un reçu, s'il vous plaît.
Could I have the check/a receipt, please?

Pouvons-nous payer chacun notre part?
Can we pay separately?

Où sont les toilettes, s'il vous plaît?
Where are the restrooms, please?

---

la restauration rapide • fast food

la paille
straw

le hamburger
burger

la boisson non-
alcoolisée
soft drink

les frites
french fries

la serviette en
papier
paper napkin

le plateau
tray

le hamburger avec des frites
burger meal

la pizza
pizza

le tarif
price list

la boisson en boîte
canned drink

la livraison à domicile
home delivery

le marchand de hot-dogs
hot dog vendor

vocabulaire • vocabulary

la pizzeria
pizzeria

le restaurant rapide
burger bar

la carte
menu

manger sur place
for here

à emporter
to go

réchauffer
reheat (v)

le ketchup
ketchup

À emporter, s'il vous plaît.
Can I have that to go, please?

Est-ce que vous livrez à domicile?
Do you deliver?

le petit pan
bun

la moutarde
mustard

la saucisse
sausage

le hamburger
hamburger

le hamburger au poulet
chicken burger

le hamburger végétarien
veggie burger

le hot-dog
hot dog

la garniture
filling

le sandwich
sandwich

le sandwich mixte
club sandwich

le canapé
open sandwich

le taco
wrap

la sauce
sauce

salé
savory

sucré
sweet

la garniture
topping

le kébab
kebab

les beignets de poulet
chicken nuggets

les crêpes | crêpes

le poisson avec des frites
fish and chips

les côtes
ribs

le poulet frit
fried chicken

la pizza
pizza

le petit déjeuner • breakfast

le lait
milk

les céréales
cereal

la confiture
jam

les fruit secs
dried fruit

le jambon
ham

le fromage
cheese

le biscuit
scandinave
crispbread

le buffet du petit déjeuner
breakfast buffet

la confiture
d'oranges
marmalade

le pâté
pâté

le beurre
butter

le jus de fruit
fruit juice

le café
coffee

le chocolat chaud
hot chocolate

le croissant
croissant

le thé
tea

la table du petit déjeuner | breakfast table

les boissons | drinks

la tomate
tomato

le boudin
black pudding

le toast
toast

la saucisse
sausage

l'œuf sur
le plat
fried egg

le bacon
bacon

le petit déjeuner anglais
English breakfast

la brioche
brioche

le pain
bread

le jaune d'œuf
yolk

les kippers
kippers

le pain perdu
French toast

l'œuf à la coque
boiled egg

les œufs brouillés
scrambled eggs

la crème
cream

le yaourt aux fruits
fruit yogurt

les crêpes
crêpes

les gaufres
waffles

le porridge
oatmeal

les fruits
fresh fruit

le repas • dinner

le potage | soup

le bouillon | broth

le ragoût | stew

le curry | curry

le rôti
roast

la tourte
pie

le soufflé
soufflé

le chiche-kébab
kebab

les boulettes de viande
meatballs

l'omelette
omelet

le sauté | stir fry

les nouilles
noodles

les pâtes | pasta

le riz
rice

la salade composée
tossed salad

la salade verte
green salad

la vinaigrette
dressing

la préparation • techniques

farci | stuffed

en sauce | in sauce

grillé | grilled

mariné | marinated

poché | poached

en purée | mashed

cuit | baked

sauté | pan-fried

frit
fried

macéré
pickled

fumé
smoked

frit
deep fried

au sirop
in syrup

assaisonné
dressed

cuit à la vapeur
steamed

séché
cured

l'étude
study

l'école • school

le tableau
blackboard

l'institutrice
teacher

le cartable
schoolbag

l'élève
student

le pupitre
desk

la craie
chalk

la salle de classe | classroom

l'écolière
schoolgirl

l'écolier
schoolboy

vocabulaire • vocabulary		
l'histoire history	les sciences science	la physique physics
les langues languages	l'art/le dessin art	la chimie chemistry
la littérature literature	la musique music	la biologie biology
la géographie geography	les mathématiques math	l'éducation physique physical education

les activités • activities

lire | read (v)

écrire | write (v)

épeler
spell (v)

dessiner
draw (v)

la plume
nib

le crayon de couleur
colored pencil

le taille-
crayon
pencil
sharpener

le projecteur numérique
digital projector

le stylo
pen

le crayon
pencil

la gomme
eraser

le cahier
notebook

le livre | textbook

la trousse
pencil case

la règle
ruler

questionner
question (v)

répondre
answer (v)

discuter
discuss (v)

apprendre
learn (v)

vocabulaire • vocabulary

le directeur principal	**la réponse** answer	**la note** grade
la leçon lesson	**les devoirs** homework	**la classe** year
la question question	**l'examen** test	**le dictionnaire** dictionary
prendre des notes take notes (v)	**la rédaction** essay	**l'encyclopédie** encyclopedia

les mathématiques • math

les formes • shapes

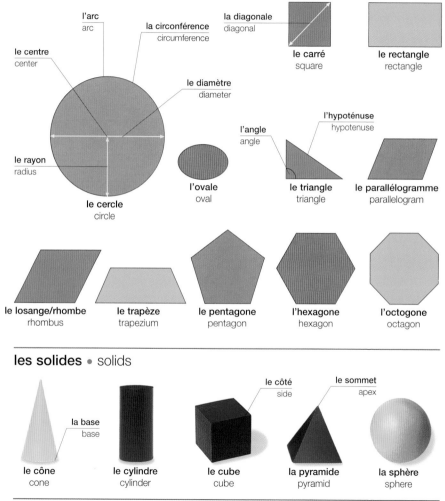

l'arc
arc

la circonférence
circumference

la diagonale
diagonal

le centre
center

le diamètre
diameter

le carré
square

le rectangle
rectangle

le rayon
radius

l'ovale
oval

l'angle
angle

l'hypoténuse
hypotenuse

le triangle
triangle

le parallélogramme
parallelogram

le cercle
circle

le losange/rhombe
rhombus

le trapèze
trapezium

le pentagone
pentagon

l'hexagone
hexagon

l'octogone
octagon

les solides • solids

la base
base

le côté
side

le sommet
apex

le cône
cone

le cylindre
cylinder

le cube
cube

la pyramide
pyramid

la sphère
sphere

les lignes • lines

droit
straight

parallèle
parallel

perpendiculaire
perpendicular

courbe
curved

les mesures • measurements

le volume
volume

le numérateur
numerator

le dénominateur
denominator

la fraction
fraction

les dimensions
dimensions

la hauteur
height

la profondeur
depth

la largeur
width

la longueur
length

l'aire
area

l'équipement • equipment

l'équerre
square

le rapporteur
protractor

la règle
ruler

le compas
compass

la calculatrice
calculator

---

vocabulaire • vocabulary

la géométrie geometry	**plus** plus	**fois** times	**égale(nt)** equals	**additionner** add (v)	**multiplier** multiply (v)	**l'équation** equation
l'arithmétique arithmetic	**moins** minus	**divisé par** divided by	**compter** count (v)	**soustraire** subtract (v)	**diviser** divide (v)	**le pourcentage** percentage

la science • science

le laboratoire
laboratory

la balance
scales

le poids
weight

la balance à ressort
spring balance

le creuset
crucible

le bec Bunsen
bunsen burner

le trépied
tripod

le statif
clamp stand

la bouteille
glass bottle

l'éprouvette
test tube

le support
rack

la pince
clamp

l'entonnoir
funnel

le bouchon
stopper

le chronomètre
timer

la fiole
flask

la boîte de Pétri
petri dish

l'expérience | experiment

le thermomètre
thermometer

la seringue
syringe

la pince fine
tweezers

le scalpel
scalpel

le compte-gouttes
dropper

le forceps | forceps

la pince
tongs

la spatule
spatula

le pilon
pestle

le mortier
mortar

le papier filtre
filter paper

les lunettes de
protection
safety goggles

l'oculaire
eyepiece

le bouton de
mise au point
focusing knob

la lentille de
l'objectif
objective lens

la tige de verre
glass stirrer

la pipette
pipette

le bécher
beaker

la platine
stage

le porte-objet
slide

l'aimant
magnet

la pince crocodile
alligator clip

le miroir
mirror

l'électrode négative
negative electrode

l'électrode
positive
positive
electrode

le microscope | microscope

la pile | battery

l'enseignement supérieur • college

le secrétariat
admissions
office

le terrain
de sport
sports field

le restaurant
universitaire
cafeteria

la résidence
universitaire
residence hall

le service
de santé
clinic

le campus | campus

vocabulaire • vocabulary

la carte de lecteur library card	**les renseignements** help desk	**le prêt** loan
la salle de lecture reading room	**emprunter** borrow (v)	**le livre** book
	réserver reserve (v)	**le titre** title
les ouvrages recommandés reading list	**renouveler** renew (v)	**le couloir** aisle
la date de retour due date		

la bibliothécaire
librarian

le service de prêt
circulation desk

les rayons
bookshelves

le périodique
periodical

la revue
journal

la bibliothèque | library

l'étudiant
undergraduate

l'assistant
professor

la licenciée
graduate

la robe
robe

la salle de cours
lecture hall

la cérémonie de la remise des diplômes
graduation ceremony

les écoles • schools

le modèle
model

l'école des beaux arts
art college

le Conservatoire
music school

l'école de danse
dance academy

vocabulaire • vocabulary

la bourse scholarship	**la recherche** research	**la dissertation** dissertation	**la médecine** medicine	**la philosophie** philosophy
le diplôme diploma	**la maîtrise** master's degree	**l'U.F.R.** department	**la zoologie** zoology	**la littérature** literature
la licence degree	**le doctorat** doctorate	**le droit** law	**la physique** physics	**l'histoire d'art** art history
de troisième cycle postgraduate	**la thèse** thesis	**les études d'ingénieur** engineering	**les sciences politiques** politics	**les sciences économiques** economics

le travail
work

le bureau 1 • office 1

la corbeille
arrivée
in-tray

le moniteur
monitor

le porte-crayons
desktop organizer

le carnet
notebook

le portable
laptop

la corbeille
départ
out-tray

le tiroir
drawer

le bureau
desk

la chaise
tournante
swivel chair

la corbeille à
papier
wastebasket

le meuble-classeur
filing cabinet

---

l'équipement de bureau • office equipment

le magasin à
papier
paper tray

l'imprimante | printer

le fax | fax machine

vocabulaire • vocabulary	
imprimer print (v)	**agrandir** enlarge (v)
photocopier copy (v)	**réduire** reduce (v)

J'ai besoin de faire des photocopies.
I need to make some copies.

---

les fournitures de bureau • office supplies

la fiche compliments
notecard

l'en-tête
stationery

l'enveloppe
envelope

le dossier-classeur
box file

l'étiquette
tab

la fiche intercalaire
divider

le clipboard
clipboard

le bloc-notes
notepad

le dossier suspendu
hanging file

le porte-dossiers
accordion file

le classeur à levier
ring binder

les agrafes
staples

le scotch
tape

le tampon encreur
ink pad

l'agenda
personal organizer

l'agrafeuse
stapler

le dévidoir de scotch
tape dispenser

le perforateur
hole punch

le cachet
rubber stamp

l'élastique
rubber band

la pince à dessin
bulldog clip

le trombone
paper clip

la punaise
thumbtack

le panneau d'affichage | notice board

le bureau 2 • office 2

le tableau à feuilles mobiles
flipchart

le chevalet
easel

la proposition
proposal

le compte rendu
minutes

le rapport
report

le directeur
manager

le cadre
executive

le réunion | meeting

vocabulaire • vocabulary

la salle de conférence meeting room	**assister à** attend (v)
l'ordre du jour agenda	**présider** chair (v)

La conférence est à quelle heure?
What time is the meeting?

Quelles sont vos heures de bureau?
What are your office hours?

la conférencière
speaker

la présentation | presentation

les affaires • business

l'homme d'affaires
businessman

la femme d'affaires
businesswoman

le déjeuner d'affaires
business lunch

le voyage d'affaires
business trip

le rendez-vous
appointment

le directeur général
CEO

la cliente
client

le contrat
business deal

l'agenda | organizer

vocabulaire • vocabulary

la société company	**le personnel** staff	**la comptabilité** accounts department	**le service du contentieux** legal department
le siège social headquarters	**le salaire** salary	**le service marketing** marketing department	**le service après-vente** customer service department
la succursale regional office	**le livre de paie** payroll	**le service des ventes** sales department	**le service de ressources humaines** human resources department

l'ordinateur • computer

l'imprimante
printer

l'écran
screen

le scanneur
scanner

le portable
laptop

la touche
key

le clavier
keyboard

la souris
mouse

le haut-parleur
speaker

le matériel
hardware

la clé USB
memory stick

le disque dur externe
external hard drive

vocabulaire • vocabulary

la mémoire memory	le logiciel software	le serveur server
la RAM RAM	l'application application	le port port
les bytes bytes	le programme program	le processeur processor
le système system	le réseau network	le câble électrique power cord

l'iPad®
iPad

le smartphone
smartphone

le bureau • desktop

la barre de menus
menu bar

la barre d'outils
toolbar

le papier peint
wallpaper

la police
font

l'icône
icon

la barre
de défilement
scrollbar

la fenêtre
window

le fichier
file

le dossier
folder

la poubelle
trash

l'internet • internet

le navigateur
browser

naviguer
browse (v)

l'e-mail • email

l'adresse e-mail
email address

la boîte de
réception
inbox

le site web
website

vocabulaire • vocabulary					
connecter connect (v)	**le fournisseur d'accès** service provider	**entrer** log on (v)	**télécharger** download (v)	**envoyer** send (v)	**sauvegarder** save (v)
installer install (v)	**le compte e-mail** email account	**en ligne** on line	**la pièce jointe** attachment	**recevoir** receive (v)	**chercher** search (v)

les médias • media

le studio de télévision • television studio

le plateau
set

le présentateur
presenter

l'éclairage
light

la caméra
camera

la grue de caméra
camera crane

le cameraman
cameraman

---

vocabulaire • vocabulary

la chaîne channel	les nouvelles news	la presse press	le feuilleton soap opera	le dessin animé cartoon	en direct live
la programmation programming	le documentaire documentary	la série télévisée television series	le jeu télévisé game show	en différé prerecorded	émettre broadcast (v)

---

l'interviewer
interviewer

la reporter
reporter

le télésouffleur
teleprompter

la présentatrice
newscaster

les acteurs
actors

la perche
sound boom

la claquette
clapper board

le décor de cinéma
movie set

la radio • radio

l'ingénieur du son / sound technician

le pupitre de mixage / mixing desk

le microphone / microphone

le studio d'enregistrement | recording studio

vocabulaire • vocabulary

la station de radio radio station	**la fréquence** frequency
le D.J. DJ	**le volume** volume
l'émission broadcast	**régler** tune (v)
la longueur d'ondes wavelength	**les ondes courtes** short wave
les grandes ondes long wave	**les ondes moyennes** medium wave
analogique analog	**numérique** digital

le droit • law

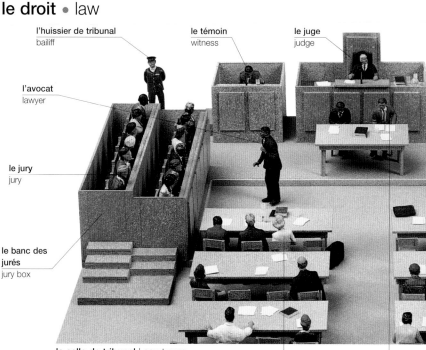

l'huissier de tribunal
bailiff

le témoin
witness

le juge
judge

l'avocat
lawyer

le jury
jury

le banc des jurés
jury box

la salle de tribunal | courtroom

l'accusation
prosecution

le greffier
clerk

---

vocabulaire • vocabulary

le cabinet lawyer's office	**l'assignation** summons	**l'acte judiciaire** writ	**la cause** court case
le conseil juridique legal advice	**la déposition** statement	**la date du procès** court date	**l'accusation** charge
le client client	**le mandat** warrant	**le plaidoyer** plea	**l'accusé** accused

---

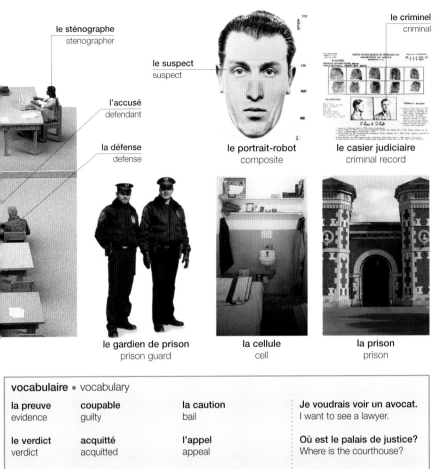

le sténographe
stenographer

le suspect
suspect

l'accusé
defendant

la défense
defense

le criminel
criminal

le portrait-robot
composite

le casier judiciaire
criminal record

le gardien de prison
prison guard

la cellule
cell

la prison
prison

---

vocabulaire • vocabulary

la preuve evidence	**coupable** guilty	**la caution** bail	**Je voudrais voir un avocat.** I want to see a lawyer.
le verdict verdict	**acquitté** acquitted	**l'appel** appeal	**Où est le palais de justice?** Where is the courthouse?
innocent innocent	**la condamnation** sentence	**la liberté conditionnelle** parole	**Est-ce que je peux verser la caution?** Can I post bail?

la ferme 1 • farm 1

l'agriculteur/le fermier
farmer

les terres cultivées
farmland

la cour de ferme
farmyard

la dépendence
outbuilding

la maison d'habitation
farmhouse

le champ
field

la grange
barn

le potager
vegetable garden

la haie
hedge

la barrière
gate

la clôture
fence

le pré
pasture

le bétail
livestock

le cultivateur
cultivator

le tracteur | tractor

la moissonneuse-batteuse | combine

les exploitations agricoles • types of farm

la culture
crop

la ferme de culture
crop farm

la ferme laitière
dairy farm

le troupeau
flock

la ferme d'élevage de
moutons
sheep farm

la ferme d'aviculture
poultry farm

la ferme d'élevage
porcin
pig farm

le centre de
pisciculture
fish farm

l'exploitation fruitière
fruit farm

la vigne
vine

la vigne
vineyard

les activités • actions

le sillon
furrow

labourer
plow (v)

semer
sow (v)

traire
milk (v)

donner à manger
feed (v)

arroser | water (v)

récolter | harvest (v)

vocabulaire • vocabulary		
l'herbicide herbicide	**le troupeau** herd	**l'auge** trough
le pesticide pesticide	**le silo** silo	**planter** plant (v)

la ferme 2 • farm 2

les cultures • crops

le blé
wheat

le maïs
corn

l'orge
barley

le colza
rapeseed

le tournesol
sunflower

la balle
bale

le foin
hay

la luzerne
alfalfa

le tabac
tobacco

le riz
rice

le thé
tea

le café
coffee

le lin
flax

la canne à sucre
sugarcane

le coton
cotton

l'épouvantail
scarecrow

le bétail • livestock

le porcelet
piglet

le cochon
pig

le veau
calf

la vache
cow

le taureau
bull

le mouton
sheep

l'agneau
lamb

le chevreau
kid

la chèvre
goat

le cheval
horse

le poulain
foal

l'âne
donkey

le poussin
chick

le poulet
chicken

le coq
rooster

le dindon
turkey

le caneton
duckling

le canard
duck

l'écurie
stable

l'enclos
pen

le poulailler
chicken coop

la porcherie
pig sty

la construction • construction

l'échafaudage
scaffolding

l'échelle
ladder

la fenêtre
window

le chevron
rafter

la palette
pallet

le chariot de levage
forklift truck

le chantier
building site

le linteau
lintel

le mur
wall

la poutre
girder

le casque de
sécurité
hard hat

la ceinture à outils
toolbelt

la poutre
beam

le ciment
cement

construire
build (v)

le maçon
construction worker

la bétonnière
cement mixer

les matériaux • materials

la brique
brick

le bois
lumber

la tuile
roof tile

le bloc de béton
concrete block

les outils • tools

le mortier
mortar

la truelle
trowel

le niveau à bulle
level

le manche
handle

le marteau de forgeron
sledgehammer

la pioche
pickax

la pelle
shovel

les machines •

machinery

le rouleau compresseur
roller

le tombereau
dump truck

le support
support

le crochet
hook

la grue | crane

les travaux • roadworks

le macadam goudronné
asphalt

le cône
cone

le marteau-piqueur
jackhammer

le revêtement
resurfacing

la pelle mécanique
excavator

les professions 1 • occupations 1

le menuisier
carpenter

l'électricien
electrician

le plombier
plumber

le maçon
construction worker

le jardinier
gardener

l'aspirateur
vacuum
cleaner

le nettoyeur
cleaner

le mécanicien
mechanic

le boucher
butcher

le coiffeur
hairdresser

la marchande de
poissons
fish-seller

le marchand de
légumes
produce-seller

la fleuriste
florist

le coiffeur
barber

le bijoutier
jeweler

l'employée de magasin
sales clerk

l'agent immobilier
realtor

l'opticien
optician

le masque
mask

la dentiste
dentist

le docteur
doctor

la pharmacienne
pharmacist

l'infirmière
nurse

la vétérinaire
veterinarian

le fermier
farmer

le pêcheur
fisherman

la mitrailleuse
machine gun

le badge
badge

l'uniforme
uniform

le garde
security guard

le marin
sailor

le soldat
soldier

le policier
police officer

le pompier
firefighter

les professions 2 • occupations 2

l'avocat
lawyer

le comptable
accountant

la maquette
model

l'architecte
architect

la scientifique
scientist

l'institutrice
teacher

le bibliothécaire
librarian

la réceptionniste
receptionist

le sac
postal
mailbag

le facteur
mail carrier

le conducteur de bus
bus driver

le camionneur
truck driver

le chauffeur de taxi
cab driver

le pilote
pilot

l'hôtesse de l'air
flight attendant

l'agent de voyages
travel agent

la toque
chef's hat

le chef
chef

le tutu
tutu

le musicien
musician

la danseuse
dancer

la comédienne
actress

la chanteuse
singer

la serveuse
waitress

le barman
bartender

le sportif
sportsman

le sculpteur
sculptor

les notes
notes

la peintre
painter

le photographe
photographer

la présentatrice
newscaster

le journaliste
journalist

la rédactrice
editor

le dessinateur
designer

la couturière
seamstress

le couturier
tailor

le transport
transportation

les routes • roads

l'autoroute
freeway

le poste de
péage
toll booth

les signalisations
road markings

la bretelle
d'accès
frontage
road

à sens unique
one-way

l'îlot directionnel
divider

le carrefour
interchange

les feux
traffic light

la file de droite
right lane

la voie centrale
center lane

la voie de
dépassement
passing lane

la bretelle de sortie
exit ramp

la circulation
traffic

l'autopont
overpass

l'accotement
stabilisé
shoulder

le camion
truck

le terre-plein
median strip

le passage inférieur
underpass

le passage clouté
crosswalk

le téléphone de secours
emergency phone

le parking réservé aux personnes handicapées
disabled parking

l'embouteillage
traffic jam

le GPS
satnav

le parc-mètre
parking meter

l'agent de la circulation
traffic policeman

vocabulaire • vocabulary

le rond-point roundabout	**garer** park (v)	**remorquer** tow away (v)
la déviation detour	**doubler** pass (v)	**la route à quatre voies** divided highway
les travaux road work	**conduire** drive (v)	**C'est la route pour...?** Is this the road to...?
la glissière de sécurité guard rail	**faire marche arrière** back up (v)	**Où peut-on se garer?** Where can I park?

les panneaux routiers • road signs

sens interdit
do not enter

la limitation de vitesse
speed limit

danger
hazard

arrêt interdit
no stopping

interdit de tourner à droite
no right turn

le bus • bus

le siège du conducteur
driver's seat

la poignée
handrail

la porte automatique
automatic door

la roue avant
front wheel

le compartiment à bagages
luggage hold

la porte | door

le car | long-distance bus

les types de bus • types of buses

le numéro de bus
route number

le conducteur
driver

le bus à deux étages
double-decker bus

le tramway
tram

le trolleybus
trolley bus

le bus scolaire | school bus

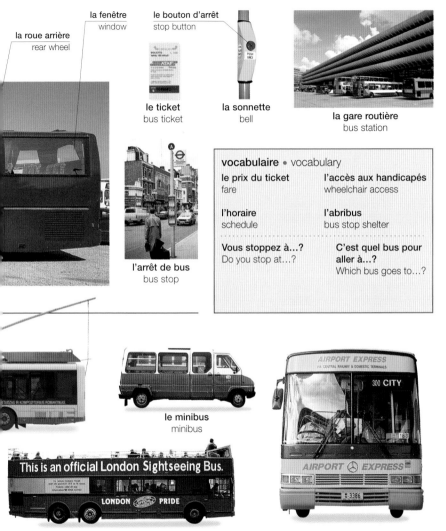

la roue arrière
rear wheel

la fenêtre
window

le bouton d'arrêt
stop button

le ticket
bus ticket

la sonnette
bell

la gare routière
bus station

l'arrêt de bus
bus stop

vocabulaire • vocabulary

le prix du ticket	**l'accès aux handicapés**
fare	wheelchair access
l'horaire	**l'abribus**
schedule	bus stop shelter
Vous stoppez à…?	**C'est quel bus pour**
Do you stop at…?	**aller à…?**
	Which bus goes to…?

le minibus
minibus

le bus de touristes | tour bus

la navette | shuttle bus

la voiture 1 • car 1

l'extérieur • exterior

le rétroviseur
side mirror

le pare-brise
windshield

le rétroviseur
rearview mirror

l'essuie-glace
windshield wiper

la porte
door

le capot
hood

le coffre
trunk

le clignotant
turn signal

le pare-chocs
bumper

le phare
headlight

la roue
wheel

le pneu
tire

la plaque d'immatriculation
license plate

les bagages
luggage

la galerie
roof rack

le hayon
tailgate

la ceinture de
sécurité
seat belt

le siège d'enfant
car seat

les modèles · types

la voiture électrique
electric car

la berline à hayon
hatchback

la berline
sedan

le break
station wagon

la décapotable
convertible

le cabriolet sport
sports car

la voiture à six places
minivan

la quatre-quatre
four-wheel drive

la voiture d'époque
vintage

la limousine
limousine

la station-service · gas station

la pompe
gas pump

le tarif
price

l'aire de stationnement
forecourt

vocabulaire · vocabulary

l'huile oil	**avec plomb** leaded	**le lave-auto** car wash
l'essence gasoline	**le diesel** diesel	**l'antigel** antifreeze
sans plomb unleaded	**le garage** garage	**le lave-glace** washer fluid

Le plein, s'il vous plaît.
Fill it up, please.

la voiture 2 • car 2

l'intérieur • interior

le siège arrière
back seat

l'accoudoir
armrest

le repose-tête
headrest

le verrouillage
door lock

la poignée
handle

vocabulaire • vocabulary

à deux portes	à quatre portes	automatique	le frein	l'accélérateur
two-door	four-door	automatic	brake	accelerator
à trois portes	manuel	l'allumage	l'embrayage	la climatisation
hatchback	manual	ignition	clutch	air conditioning

Pouvez-vous m'indiquer la route pour…?
Can you tell me the way to…?

Où est le parking?
Where is the parking lot?

On peut se garer ici?
Can I park here?

les commandes • controls

| le volant
steering wheel | le klaxon
horn | le tableau de bord
dashboard | les feux de détresse
hazard lights | le navigateur par satellite
satellite navigation |

la conduite à gauche | left-hand drive

| le thermomètre
temperature gauge | le compte-tours
tachometer | le compteur
speedometer | la jauge d'essence
fuel gauge |

la stéréo
car stereo

l'interrupteur feux
light switch

la manette de chauffage
heater controls

l'odomètre
odometer

l'airbag
air bag

le levier de vitesses
gearshift

la conduite à droite | right-hand drive

la voiture 3 • car 3

la mécanique • mechanics

le réservoir de **lave-glace**
washer fluid reservoir

la jauge d'huile
dipstick

le filtre à air
air filter

le réservoir de liquide de frein
brake fluid reservoir

la batterie
battery

la **carrosserie**
bodywork

le réservoir de liquide de **refroidissement**
coolant reservoir

la culasse
cylinder head

le tuyau
pipe

le toit ouvrant
sunroof

le moteur
engine

le radiateur
radiator

le ventilateur
fan

l'enjoliveur
hubcap

la boîte de **vitesses**
gearbox

la transmission
transmission

l'arbre de **transmission**
driveshaft

la crevaison • flat tire

la roue de secours
spare tire

la manivelle
tire iron

les écrous de roue
wheel nuts

le cric
jack

changer une roue
change a tire (v)

le toit
roof

la suspension
suspension

le silencieux
muffler

le pot d'échappement
exhaust pipe

vocabulaire • vocabulary

l'accident de voiture
car accident

le turbocompresseur
turbocharger

la panne
breakdown

le distributeur
distributor

l'assurance
insurance

le châssis
chassis

la dépanneuse
towtruck

le frein à main
parking brake

le mécanicien
mechanic

l'alternateur
alternator

**la pression des
pneus**
tire pressure

**la courroie de
cames**
cam belt

le porte-fusibles
fuse box

**Ma voiture est en
panne.**
My car has broken
down.

la bougie
sparkplug

**la courroie de
ventilateur**
fan belt

**Ma voiture ne
démarre pas.**
My car won't start.

**le réservoir
d'essence**
gas tank

**Faites-vous les
réparations?**
Do you do repairs?

**le réglage de
l'allumage**
timing

Le moteur chauffe
The engine is
overheating

la moto • motorcycle

le casque
helmet

le clignotant
turn signal

le compteur
speedometer

le frein
brake

l'embrayage
clutch

le klaxon
horn

l'accélérateur
throttle

les commandes
controls

le porte-bagages
carrier

le réflecteur
reflector

le siège arrière
pillion

la selle
seat

le moteur
engine

le réservoir
d'essence
fuel tank

le feu arrière
taillight

le pot
d'échappement
exhaust pipe

le silencieux
muffler

le réservoir d'huile
oil tank

la boîte de vitesses
gearbox

le filtre d'air
air filter

la visière
visor

le vêtement en cuir
leathers

la bande
fluorescente
reflector strap

la genouillère
knee pad

les vêtements | clothing

le phare
headlight

la suspension
suspension

le garde-boue
mudguard

la pédale de frein
brake pedal

l'essieu
axle

le pneu
tire

les types • types

la moto de course | racing bike

le pare-brise
windshield

la moto routière | tourer

la moto tout-terrain | dirt bike

la béquille
stand

le scooter | scooter

la bicyclette • bicycle

la selle
saddle

le tube porte-selle
seat post

la bouteille d'eau
water bottle

le cadre
frame

le frein
brake

le moyeu
hub

les vitesses
gears

la jante
rim

le pneu
tire

la pédale
pedal

la roue dentée
cog

la chaîne
chain

le tandem
tandem

le vélo de course
racing bike

le vélo tout-terrain
mountain bike

le casque
helmet

le vélo de randonnée
touring bike

le vélo de ville
road bike

la piste cyclable | bike lane

la barre
crossbar

le guidon
handlebar

le levier de vitesse
gear lever

le levier de frein
brake lever

le démonte-pneu
tire lever

la rustine
patch

la boîte d'outils | repair kit

la fourche
fork

la clef
key

le rayon
spoke

la pompe
pump

l'antivol
lock

la roue
wheel

la valve
valve

la bande de roulement
tread

la chambre à air
inner tube

le siège d'enfant
child seat

---

vocabulaire • vocabulary

le phare headlight	**la béquille** kickstand	**le patin de frein** brake block	**le panier** basket	**le cale-pied** toe clip	**freiner** brake (v)
le feu arrière rear light	**la galerie à vélo** bike rack	**le câble** cable	**la dynamo** dynamo	**la lanière** toe strap	**faire du vélo** cycle (v)
le cataphote reflector	**les roues d'entraînement** training wheels	**le pignon** sprocket	**la crevaison** flat tire	**pédaler** pedal (v)	**changer de vitesse** change gears (v)

---

le train • train

la voiture
car

le quai
platform

le caddie
cart

le numéro de
voie
platform number

le voyageur
commuter

la gare | train station

les types de trains • types of train

la cabine du
conducteur
engineer's
cab

le rail
rail

la locomotive
engine

le train à vapeur
steam train

le train diesel | diesel train

le train électrique
electric train

le train à grande vitesse
high-speed train

le monorail
monorail

le métro
subway

le tram
tram

le train de marchandises
freight train

le porte-bagages
luggage rack

la fenêtre
window

la voie ferrée
track

la porte
door

le siège
seat

le portillon
ticket gate

le compartiment
compartment

le haut-parleur
public address system

l'horaire
schedule

le billet
ticket

la voiture-restaurant | dining car

le compartiment-couchettes
sleeping compartment

le hall de gare | concourse

vocabulaire · vocabulary

le réseau ferroviaire rail network	**le plan de métro** subway map	**le guichet** ticket office	**le rail conducteur** live rail
le rapide express train	**le retard** delay	**le contrôleur** ticket inspector	**le signal** signal
l'heure de pointe rush hour	**le prix** fare	**changer** change trains (v)	**la manette de secours** emergency lever

l'avion • aircraft

l'avion de ligne • airliner

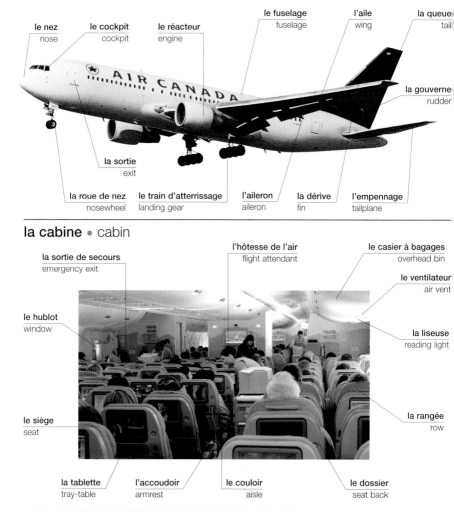

le fuselage
fuselage

l'aile
wing

la queue
tail

le nez
nose

le cockpit
cockpit

le réacteur
engine

la gouverne
rudder

la sortie
exit

la roue de nez
nosewheel

le train d'atterrissage
landing gear

l'aileron
aileron

la dérive
fin

l'empennage
tailplane

la cabine • cabin

l'hôtesse de l'air
flight attendant

le casier à bagages
overhead bin

la sortie de secours
emergency exit

le ventilateur
air vent

le hublot
window

la liseuse
reading light

la rangée
row

le siège
seat

la tablette
tray-table

l'accoudoir
armrest

le couloir
aisle

le dossier
seat back

l'U.L.M.
ultralight

le planeur
glider

le biplan
biplane

l'hélice
propeller

la montgolfière
hot-air balloon

l'avion léger
light aircraft

l'hydravion
sea plane

le missile
missile

le jet privé
private jet

le chasseur
fighter plane

la pale de rotor
rotor blade

l'hélicoptère
helicopter

le bombardier
bomber

vocabulaire • vocabulary

le pilote pilot	**décoller** take off (v)	**atterrir** land (v)	**la classe économique** economy class	**les bagages à main** carry-on luggage
le copilote copilot	**voler** fly (v)	**l'altitude** altitude	**la classe affaires** business class	**la ceinture de sécurité** seat belt

l'aéroport • airport

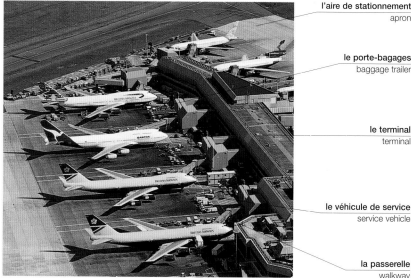

l'aire de stationnement
apron

le porte-bagages
baggage trailer

le terminal
terminal

le véhicule de service
service vehicle

la passerelle
walkway

l'avion de ligne | airliner

---

vocabulaire • vocabulary

la piste runway	**le numéro de vol** flight number	**le tapis roulant** carousel	**les vacances** vacation
le vol international international flight	**l'immigration** immigration	**la sécurité** security	**enregistrer** check in (v)
le vol domestique domestic flight	**la douane** customs	**la machine de rayons x** X-ray machine	**la tour de contrôle** control tower
la correspondance connection	**l'excédent de bagages** excess baggage	**la brochure de vacances** travel brochure	**faire une réservation de vol** make a flight reservation (v)

les bagages à main
carry-on luggage

les bagages
luggage

le chariot
cart

l'enregistrement des bagages
check-in desk

le visa
visa

le passeport | passport

la carte d'embarquement
boarding pass

le contrôle de passeports
passport control

le billet
ticket

le numéro de la porte d'embarquement
gate number

les départs
departures

la salle de départ
departure lounge

la destination
destination

les arrivées
arrivals

l'écran d'information
information screen

la boutique hors taxes
duty-free shop

le retrait des bagages
baggage claim

la station de taxis
taxi stand

la location de voitures
car rental

le navire • ship

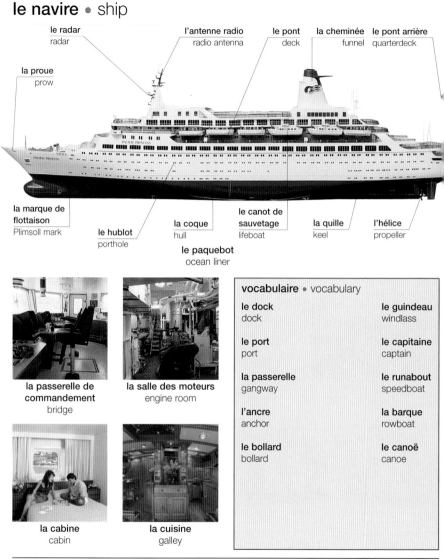

le radar
radar

l'antenne radio
radio antenna

le pont
deck

la cheminée
funnel

le pont arrière
quarterdeck

la proue
prow

la marque de
flottaison
Plimsoll mark

le hublot
porthole

la coque
hull

le canot de
sauvetage
lifeboat

la quille
keel

l'hélice
propeller

le paquebot
ocean liner

la passerelle de
commandement
bridge

la salle des moteurs
engine room

la cabine
cabin

la cuisine
galley

vocabulaire • vocabulary

le dock
dock

le port
port

la passerelle
gangway

l'ancre
anchor

le bollard
bollard

le guindeau
windlass

le capitaine
captain

le runabout
speedboat

la barque
rowboat

le canoë
canoe

autres bateaux • other ships

le ferry
ferry

le hors-bord
outboard motor

le canot pneumatique
inflatable dinghy

l'hydroptère
hydrofoil

le yacht
yacht

le catamaran
catamaran

le remorqueur
tugboat

l'aéroglisseur
hovercraft

le navire porte-conteneurs
container ship

le gréement
rigging

la cale
hold

le voilier
sailboat

le cargo
freighter

le pétrolier
oil tanker

le porte-avions
aircraft carrier

le navire de guerre
battleship

le kiosque
conning tower

le sous-marin
submarine

le port • port

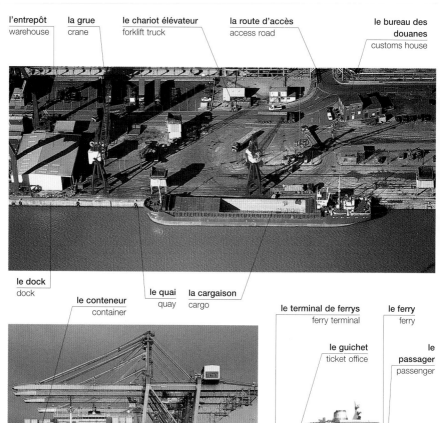

l'entrepôt
warehouse

la grue
crane

le chariot élévateur
forklift truck

la route d'accès
access road

le bureau des
douanes
customs house

le dock
dock

le conteneur
container

le quai
quay

la cargaison
cargo

le terminal de ferrys
ferry terminal

le ferry
ferry

le guichet
ticket office

le
passager
passenger

le port de conteneurs | container port

le port de passagers | passenger port

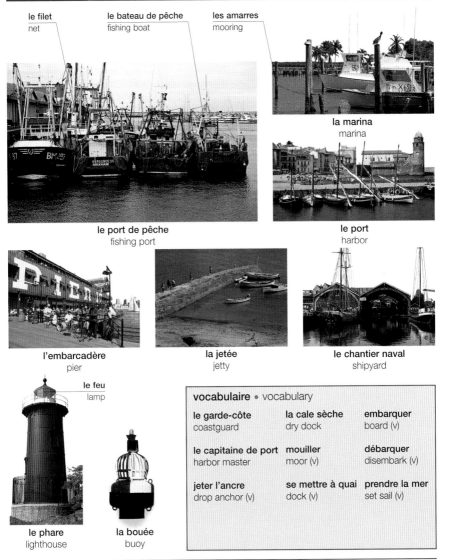

le filet
net

le bateau de pêche
fishing boat

les amarres
mooring

la marina
marina

le port de pêche
fishing port

le port
harbor

l'embarcadère
pier

la jetée
jetty

le chantier naval
shipyard

le feu
lamp

le phare
lighthouse

la bouée
buoy

vocabulaire • vocabulary

le garde-côte	la cale sèche	embarquer
coastguard	dry dock	board (v)
le capitaine de port	mouiller	débarquer
harbor master	moor (v)	disembark (v)
jeter l'ancre	se mettre à quai	prendre la mer
drop anchor (v)	dock (v)	set sail (v)

les sports
sports

le football américain • football

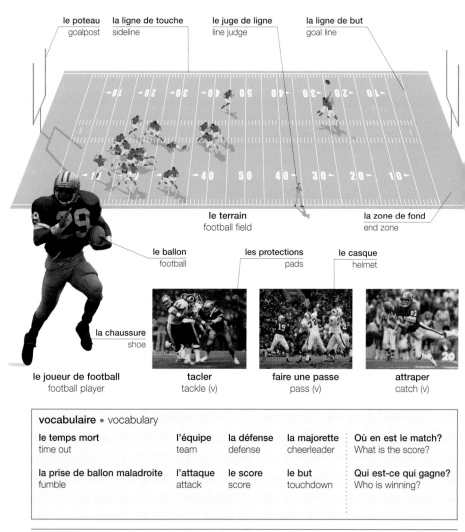

le poteau / goalpost

la ligne de touche / sideline

le juge de ligne / line judge

la ligne de but / goal line

le terrain / football field

la zone de fond / end zone

le ballon / football

les protections / pads

le casque / helmet

la chaussure / shoe

le joueur de football / football player

tacler / tackle (v)

faire une passe / pass (v)

attraper / catch (v)

vocabulaire • vocabulary

le temps mort time out	**l'équipe** team	**la défense** defense	**la majorette** cheerleader	**Où en est le match?** What is the score?
la prise de ballon maladroite fumble	**l'attaque** attack	**le score** score	**le but** touchdown	**Qui est-ce qui gagne?** Who is winning?

le rugby • rugby

le but
goal

la surface de but
in-goal area

la ligne de touche
touch line

le drapeau
flag

la ligne de ballon
mort
dead ball line

le terrain de rugby | rugby field

le ballon
ball

le maillot de
rugby
rugby uniform

botter
kick (v)

faire une passe
pass (v)

lancer
throw (v)

tacler
tackle (v)

l'essai
try

le joueur
player

la mêlée ouverte | ruck

la mêlée | scrum

le football • soccer

le ballon
football

l'avant
forward

l'arbitre
referee

le cercle central
center circle

le gardien de but
goalkeeper

la tenue
soccer
uniform

le joueur de foot
soccer player

le terrain
football field

le poteau
goalpost

le filet
net

la barre
transversale
crossbar

dribbler | dribble (v)

faire une tête
head (v)

le mur
wall

le but | goal

le coup franc | free kick

la surface de
réparation
penalty area

la ligne de but
goal line

la surface de but
goal area

le but
goal

le défenseur
defender

le juge de ligne
linesman

le drapeau de coin
corner flag

la rentrée en touche
throw-in

botter
kick (v)

la chaussure
shoe

faire une passe
pass (v)

shooter
shoot (v)

sauver
save (v)

tacler
tackle (v)

---

vocabulaire • vocabulary

le stade stadium	**la faute** foul	**le carton jaune** yellow card	**le championnat** league	**la prolongation** extra time
marquer un but score a goal (v)	**le corner** corner	**l'hors-jeu** off-side	**l'égalité** draw	**le remplaçant** substitute
le penalty penalty	**le carton rouge** red card	**l'expulsion** send off	**la mi-temps** half time	**le remplacement** substitution

---

le hockey • hockey

le hockey sur glace • ice hockey

la zone de défense
defending zone

la ligne de but
goal line

la zone
d'attaque
attack zone

la zone neutre
neutral zone

le gardien de but
goalkeeper

le but
goal

le cercle de
mise en jeu
face-off circle

le cercle central
center circle

le gant
glove

la protection
pad

le patin à
glace
ice-skate

la patinoire
ice hockey rink

la crosse
stick

le palet
puck

le hockeyeur | ice hockey player

le hockey • field hockey

la crosse de hockey
hockey stick

la balle
ball

patiner
skate (v)

frapper
hit (v)

le cricket • cricket

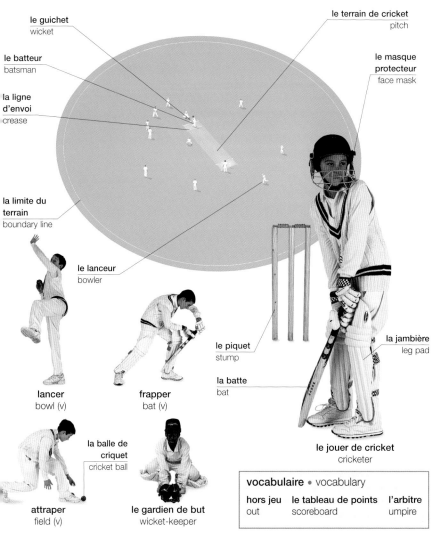

le guichet
wicket

le terrain de cricket
pitch

le batteur
batsman

le masque
protecteur
face mask

la ligne
d'envoi
crease

la limite du
terrain
boundary line

le lanceur
bowler

le piquet
stump

la jambière
leg pad

la batte
bat

lancer
bowl (v)

frapper
bat (v)

le jouer de cricket
cricketer

la balle de
criquet
cricket ball

attraper
field (v)

le gardien de but
wicket-keeper

vocabulaire • vocabulary		
hors jeu	le tableau de points	l'arbitre
out	scoreboard	umpire

le basket • basketball

la ligne de touche
sideline

l'arbitre
referee

le cercle central
center circle

la ligne de lancer franc
free-throw line

la ligne de bout
endline

le terrain
court

la ligne de centre
centerline

la ligne de trois points
three-point line

le numéro
number

le panneau
backboard

le ballon
ball

l'anneau
hoop

le filet
net

le panier
basket

le joueur de basket | basketball player

vocabulaire •
vocabulary

la passe pass	**la rentrée** throw-in
la faute foul	**l'entre-deux** jump ball
le rebond rebound	**hors jeu** out of bounds

les actions • actions

lancer
throw (v)

attraper
catch (v)

tirer
shoot (v)

sauter
jump (v)

marquer
mark (v)

bloquer
block (v)

faire rebondir
dribble (v)

faire un dunk
dunk (v)

le volley • volleyball

bloquer
block (v)

le filet
net

faire une manchette
dig (v)

l'arbitre
referee

la genouillère
knee support

le terrain | court

le baseball • baseball

le terrain • field

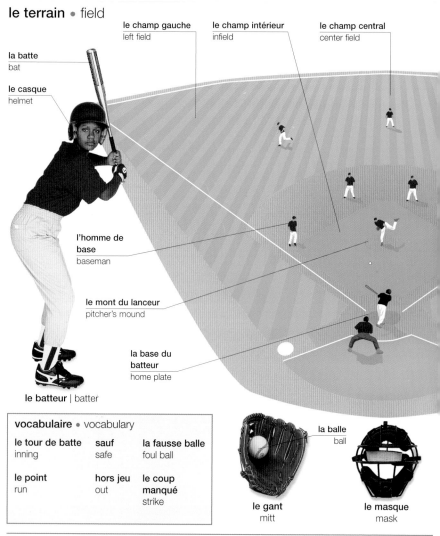

le champ gauche
left field

le champ intérieur
infield

le champ central
center field

la batte
bat

le casque
helmet

l'homme de base
baseman

le mont du lanceur
pitcher's mound

la base du batteur
home plate

le batteur | batter

la balle
ball

le gant
mitt

le masque
mask

---

vocabulaire • vocabulary

le tour de batte inning	**sauf** safe	**la fausse balle** foul ball
le point run	**hors jeu** out	**le coup manqué** strike

---

les actions • actions

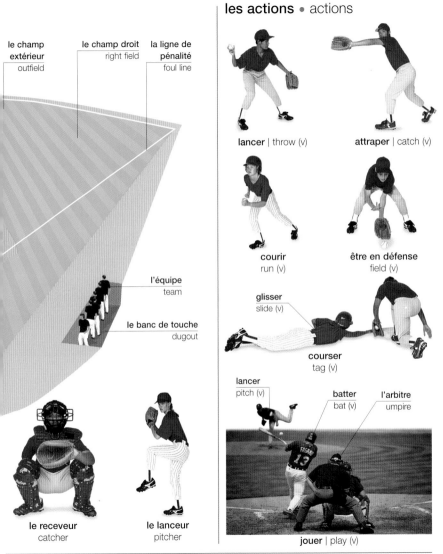

le champ
extérieur
outfield

le champ droit
right field

la ligne de
pénalité
foul line

l'équipe
team

le banc de touche
dugout

lancer | throw (v)

attraper | catch (v)

courir
run (v)

être en défense
field (v)

glisser
slide (v)

courser
tag (v)

lancer
pitch (v)

batter
bat (v)

l'arbitre
umpire

le receveur
catcher

le lanceur
pitcher

jouer | play (v)

le tennis • tennis

le manche / handle

la tête / head

la corde / string

l'arbitre / umpire

la ligne de fond / baseline

la raquette / racket

la ligne de service / service line

la ligne de côté / sideline

la balle / ball

le poignet / wristband

le court de tennis | tennis court

---

vocabulaire • vocabulary

le simple singles	**le set** set	**l'égalité** deuce	**la faute** fault	**le slice** slice	**l'effet** spin
le double doubles	**le match** match	**l'avantage** advantage	**l'as** ace	**l'échange** rally	**le juge de ligne** linesman
le jeu game	**le tiebreak** tiebreaker	**zéro** love	**l'amorti** dropshot	**net!** let!	**le championnat** championship

---

les coups • strokes

le filet
net

le smash
smash

le ramasseur
de balles
ball boy

servir
serve (v)

les tennis
tennis shoes

le joueur
player

le service
serve

la volée
volley

le retour
return

le lob
lob

le coup droit
forehand

le revers
backhand

les jeux de raquette • racket games

le volant
shuttlecock

la raquette
paddle

le badminton
badminton

le tennis de table
table tennis

le squash
squash

le racquetball
racketball

le golf • golf

le trou
hole

le départ
teeing ground

le green
green

le bunker
bunker

le drapeau
flag

exécuter un swing
swing (v)

le fairway
fairway

le rough
rough

l'obstacle d'eau
water hazard

le parcours de golf
golf course

le buggy
golf cart

la position
stance

la joueuse de golf | golfer

le pavillon | clubhouse

l'équipement • equipment

la balle de golf
golf ball

le tee
tee

le sac de golf
golf bag

les pointes
spikes

le gant
glove

le caddie
cart

la chaussure de golf
golf shoe

les clubs de golf • golf clubs

le bois
wood

le putter
putter

le fer
iron

la cale
wedge

les actions • actions

partir du tee
tee-off (v)

driver
drive (v)

putter
putt (v)

cocher
chip (v)

vocabulaire • vocabulary

le par par	**le over par** over par	**le handicap** handicap	**le caddie** caddy	**le swing en arrière** backswing	**le coup** stroke
le under par under par	**le trou en un** hole in one	**le tournoi** tournament	**les spectateurs** spectators	**le swing d'essai** practice swing	**la ligne de jeu** line of play

l'athlétisme • track and field

le couloir
lane

la piste
track

la ligne d'arrivée
finish line

la ligne de départ
starting line

le terrain
field

l'athlète
athlete

le bloc de départ
starting blocks

le sprinter
sprinter

le disque
discus

le lancement du poids
shotput

le javelot
javelin

vocabulaire • vocabulary

la course race	le record record	le photo-finish photo finish	le saut à la perche pole vault
le temps time	battre un record break a record (v)	le marathon marathon	le record personnel personal best

le chronomètre
stopwatch

le bâton
baton

la barre
crossbar

le relais
relay race

le saut en hauteur
high jump

le saut en longueur
long jump

les haies
hurdles

la gymnastique • gymnastics

le tremplin
springboard

la gymnaste
gymnast

le cheval
horse

le salto
somersault

la poutre
beam

le drapeau
ribbon

le tapis
mat

le saut
vault

les exercises au sol
floor exercises

la cabriole
tumble

la gymnastique
rythmique
rhythmic gymnastics

---

vocabulaire • vocabulary

la barre fixe horizontal bar	**le cheval d'arçons** pommel horse	**les anneaux** rings	**les médailles** medals	**l'argent** silver
les barres parallèles parallel bars	**les barres asymétriques** asymmetric bars	**le podium** podium	**l'or** gold	**le bronze** bronze

---

les sports de combat • combat sports

l'adversaire
opponent

le gant
glove

le protège-tête
guard

la ceinture
belt

le taekwondo
tae kwon do

le masque
mask

le sabre
sword

le karaté
karate

le judo
judo

le kung-fu
kung fu

l'aïkido
aikido

le kendo
kendo

la boxe thaïlandaise
kickboxing

la lutte
wrestling

la boxe
boxing

les actions • actions

la chute
fall

la prise
hold

la projection
throw

l'immobilisation
pin

le coup de pied
kick

le coup de poing
punch

le coup
strike

le saut
jump

le blocage
block

le coup
chop

vocabulaire • vocabulary

le ring boxing ring	**le round** round	**le poing** fist	**la ceinture noire** black belt	**la capoeira** capoeira
les gants de boxe boxing gloves	**le combat** bout	**le knock-out** knockout	**l'autodéfense** self-defense	**le sumo** sumo wrestling
le protège-dents mouth guard	**l'entraînement** sparring	**le punching-bag** punching bag	**les arts martiaux** martial arts	**le taï chi** tai chi

la natation • swimming
l'équipement • equipment

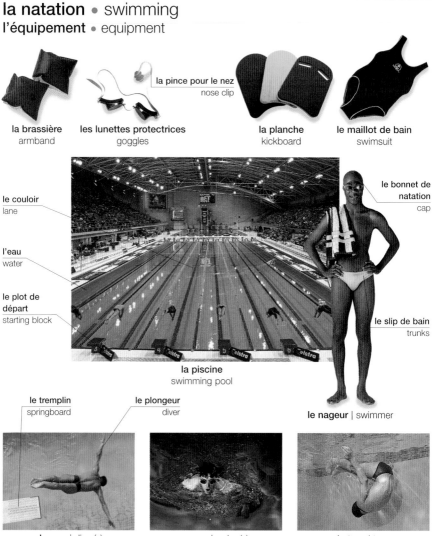

la brassière
armband

les lunettes protectrices
goggles

la pince pour le nez
nose clip

la planche
kickboard

le maillot de bain
swimsuit

le couloir
lane

l'eau
water

le plot de départ
starting block

le bonnet de natation
cap

le slip de bain
trunks

la piscine
swimming pool

le nageur | swimmer

le tremplin
springboard

le plongeur
diver

plonger | dive (v)

nager | swim (v)

le tour | turn

les styles • styles

le crawl
front crawl

la brasse
breaststroke

la nage
stroke

le coup de pied
kick

le dos crawlé | backstroke

le papillon | butterfly

la plongée • scuba diving

la combinaison
de plongée
wetsuit

la palme
flipper

la ceinture de
plomb
weight belt

la bouteille d'air
air cylinder

le masque
mask

le régulateur
regulator

le tuba
snorkel

vocabulaire • vocabulary

le plongeon dive	**nager sur place** tread water (v)	**les casiers** lockers	**le water-polo** water polo	**le petit bassin** shallow end	**la crampe** cramp
le plongeon de haut vol high dive	**le départ plongé** racing dive	**le maître nageur** lifeguard	**le grand bassin** deep end	**la nage synchronisée** synchronized swimming	**se noyer** drown (v)

la voile • sailing

le compas
compass

l'ancre
anchor

la voile d'avant
headsail

le taquet
cleat

le pont de côté
sidedeck

l'avant
bow

la barre
tiller

la coque
hull

le mât
mast

le gréement
rigging

la grand-voile
mainsail

la bôme
boom

l'arrière
stern

naviguer | navigate (v)

le yacht | yacht

la sécurité • safety

la fusée éclairante
flare

la bouée de sauvetage
life preserver

le gilet de sauvetage
life jacket

le radeau de sauvetage
life raft

les sports aquatiques • watersports

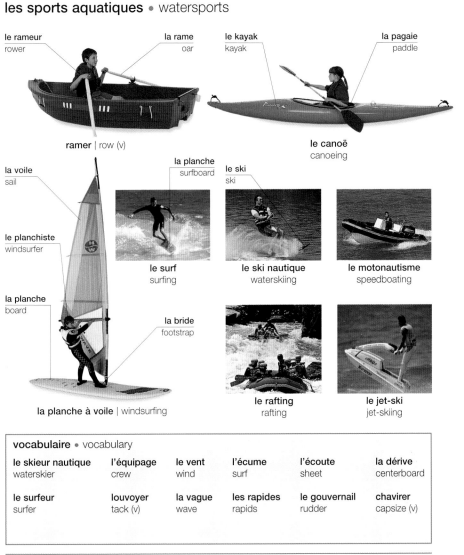

le rameur
rower

la rame
oar

le kayak
kayak

la pagaie
paddle

ramer | row (v)

le canoë
canoeing

la voile
sail

la planche
surfboard

le ski
ski

le planchiste
windsurfer

la planche
board

la bride
footstrap

le surf
surfing

le ski nautique
waterskiing

le motonautisme
speedboating

la planche à voile | windsurfing

le rafting
rafting

le jet-ski
jet-skiing

vocabulaire • vocabulary

le skieur nautique waterskier	l'équipage crew	le vent wind	l'écume surf	l'écoute sheet	la dérive centerboard
le surfeur surfer	louvoyer tack (v)	la vague wave	les rapides rapids	le gouvernail rudder	chavirer capsize (v)

l'équitation • horseback riding

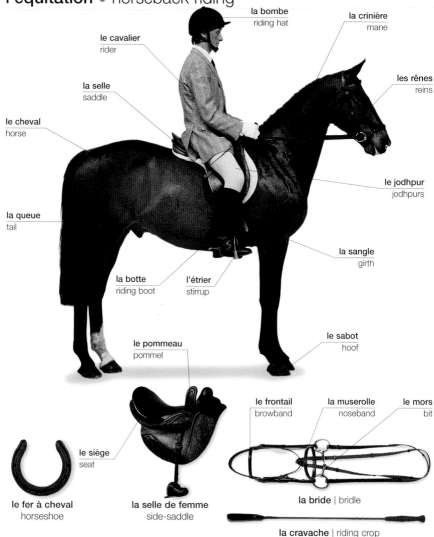

la bombe
riding hat

la crinière
mane

le cavalier
rider

les rênes
reins

la selle
saddle

le cheval
horse

le jodhpur
jodhpurs

la queue
tail

la sangle
girth

la botte
riding boot

l'étrier
stirrup

le sabot
hoof

le pommeau
pommel

le frontail
browband

la muserolle
noseband

le mors
bit

le siège
seat

le fer à cheval
horseshoe

la selle de femme
side-saddle

la bride | bridle

la cravache | riding crop

les courses • events

le cheval de course
racehorse

l'obstacle
fence

la course de chevaux
horse race

le steeple
steeplechase

la course de trot
harness race

le rodéo
rodeo

le jumping
showjumping

la course attelée
carriage race

la randonnée
trail-riding

le dressage
dressage

le polo
polo

---

vocabulaire • vocabulary

le pas walk	**le petit galop** canter	**le saut** jump	**le licou** halter	**l'enclos** paddock	**la course de plat** flat race
le trot trot	**le galop** gallop	**le valet d'écurie** groom	**l'écurie** stable	**l'arène** arena	**le champs de courses** racecourse

---

la pêche • fishing

le plomb | sinker

le barbillon
barb

l'œillet
eye

l'hameçon
fishhook

l'amorce | bait

le flotteur
float

l'appât
lure

la mouche
fly

l'épuisette
landing net

la boîte d'équipement
tackle box

la bourriche
keep net

la ligne
line

la canne à pêche
fishing rod

le moulinet
reel

**les bottes
de pêche**
waders

le pêcheur | angler

les genres de pêche • types of fishing

la pêche en eau douce
freshwater fishing

la pêche à la mouche
fly fishing

la pêche sportive
sport fishing

la pêche hauturière
deep sea fishing

**la pêche au lancer
en mer**
surfcasting

les activités • activities

lancer
cast (v)

attraper
catch (v)

ramener
reel in (v)

prendre au filet
net (v)

lâcher
release (v)

---

vocabulaire • vocabulary

amorcer bait (v)	**le matériel de pêche** tackle	**l'imperméable** rain gear	**le permis de pêche** fishing permit	**le panier de pêche** creel
mordre bite (v)	**le tambour** spool	**la perche** pole	**la pêche maritime** marine fishing	**la pêche sous-marine** spearfishing

le ski • skiing

la pente de ski
ski slope

le télésiège
chairlift

la télécabine
cable car

le gant
glove

le bâton de ski
ski pole

la pointe
tip

la carre
edge

le ski
ski

la piste de ski
ski run

la barrière de sécurité
safety barrier

la veste de ski
ski jacket

la skieuse
skier

la chaussure de ski
ski boot

les épreuves • events

la porte
gate

la descente
downhill skiing

le slalom
slalom

le saut
ski jump

le ski de randonnée
cross-country skiing

les sports d'hiver • winter sports

les lunettes de ski
goggles

**le patin
à glace**
skate

l'escalade en glace
ice climbing

le patinage
ice skating

le patinage artistique
figure skating

le surf des neiges
snowboarding

le bobsleigh
bobsled

la luge
luge

l'autoneige
snowmobile

la luge
sledding

vocabulaire • vocabulary

le ski alpin alpine skiing	**le traîneau à chiens** dog-sledding
le slalom géant giant slalom	**le patinage de vitesse** speed skating
hors piste off-piste	**le biathlon** biathlon
le curling curling	**l'avalanche** avalanche

les autres sports • other sports

le planeur
glider

le deltaplane
hang-glider

le vol plané
gliding

le parachute
parachute

le deltaplane
hang-gliding

la corde
rope

l'escalade
rock-climbing

le parachutisme
parachuting

le parapente
paragliding

le saut en chute libre
skydiving

le rappel
rappelling

le saut à l'élastique
bungee jumping

le coureur
automobile
race-car
driver

le rallye
rally driving

la course automobile
auto racing

le motocross
motocross

la course de moto
motorcycle racing

la planche à
roulettes
skateboard

la crosse
stick

le
masque
mask

le
fleuret
foil

**la planche à
roulettes**
skateboarding

le patin en ligne
inline skating

le lacrosse
lacrosse

l'escrime
fencing

la quille
pin

l'arc
bow

la cible
target

la flèche
arrow

le carquois
quiver

le tir à l'arcx
archery

le tir à cible
target shooting

la boule de
bowling
bowling ball

le bowling
bowling

le billard américain
pool

le billard
snooker

le conditionnement physique • fitness

le vélo
d'entraînement
exercise bike

l'appareil de gym
gym machine

le banc
bench

les poids
free weights

la barre
bar

le gymnase
gym

la machine
à ramer
rowing machine

le tapis roulant
treadmill

la machine de
randonnée
cross-trainer

l'entraîneuse
individuelle
personal trainer

l'escalier
d'entraînement
step machine

la piscine
swimming pool

le sauna
sauna

les exercices • exercises

l'étirement
stretch

la fente en avant
lunge

le collant
tights

la traction
push-up

l'haltère
dumbbell

la flexion de jambes
squat

le redressement
assis
sit-up

l'exercise pour
les biceps
biceps curl

la traction pour les
jambes
leg press

la barre à
poids
weight bar

les
baskets
athletic
shoes

l'exercice pour la
poitrine
chest press

l'entraînement poids
et haltères
weight training

le jogging
jogging

le Pilates
Pilates

vocabulaire • vocabulary

s'entraîner	**jogger sur place**	**étendre**	**l'aéroboxe**	**l'entraînement en circuit**
train (v)	jog in place (v)	extend (v)	boxercise	circuit training
s'échauffer	**fléchir**	**tirer**	**le saut à la corde**	
warm up (v)	flex (v)	pull up (v)	rope-jumping	

le temps libre
leisure

le théâtre • theater

le rideau
curtain

les coulisses
wings

le décor
set

le public
audience

l'orchestre
orchestra

la scène | stage

le fauteuil
seat

la deuxième galerie
upper balcony

la rangée
row

la loge
box

la corbeille
balcony

le balcon
balcony

l'allée
aisle

l'orchestre
orchestra

les places | seating

vocabulaire • vocabulary

la distribution cast	le texte script	la première opening night
l'acteur actor	la toile de fond backdrop	l'entracte intermission
l'actrice actress	le metteur en scène director	le programme program
la pièce de théâtre play	le metteur en scène producer	la fosse d'orchestre orchestra pit

le costume
costume

le concert
concert

la comédie musicale
musical

le ballet
ballet

vocabulaire • vocabulary

le placeur usher	**la bande sonore** soundtrack	**Ça commence à quelle heure?** What time does it start?
la musique classique classical music	**applaudir** applaud (v)	**Je voudrais deux billets pour la représentation de ce soir.** I'd like two tickets for tonight's performance.
la partition musical score	**le bis** encore	

l'opéra
opera

le cinéma • cinema

le pop-corn
popcorn

le foyer
lobby

la caisse
box office

l'affiche
poster

la salle de cinéma
movie theater

l'écran
screen

vocabulaire • vocabulary

la comédie comedy	**la comédie romantique** romance
le thriller thriller	**le film de science-fiction** science fiction movie
le film d'horreur horror movie	**le film d'aventures** adventure
le western Western	**le film d'animation** animated film

l'orchestre • orchestra

les cordes • strings

la harpe
harp

le chef d'orchestre
conductor

le contrebasse
double bass

le violon
violin

le podium
podium

l'alto
viola

le violoncelle
cello

la partition
score

la clé de sol
treble clef

la note
note

la portée
staff

la clé de fa
bass clef

Andante

le piano | piano

la notation | notation

---

vocabulaire • vocabulary

l'ouverture overture	la sonate sonata	le silence rest	le dièse sharp	le bécarre natural	la gamme scale
la symphonie symphony	les instruments instruments	le ton pitch	le bémol flat	la barre de mesure bar	la baguette baton

---

les bois • woodwind

le piccolo
piccolo

la flûte traversière
flute

le hautbois
oboe

le cor anglais
English horn

la clarinette
clarinet

la clarinette
bass clarinet

le basson
bassoon

le contrebasson
double bassoon

le saxophone
saxophone

la percussion • percussion

le vibraphone
vibraphone

les bongos
bongos

la caisse claire
snare drum

la timbale
kettle drum

le gong
gong

les cymbales
cymbals

le tambour
tambourine

le triangle
triangle

les maracas
maracas

les pédales
foot pedals

les cuivres • brass

la trompette
trumpet

le trombone
trombone

le cor
French horn

le tuba
tuba

le concert • concert

le haut-parleur
speaker

les fans
fans

le chanteur
lead singer

le guitariste
guitarist

le microphone
microphone

le batteur
drummer

le concert de rock | rock concert

les instruments • instruments

le pick-up
pickup

le manche
neck

la basse
bass guitar

le piano électronique
keyboard

le chevalet
bridge

le sillet
fret

la cheville
tuning peg

la corde
string

le tambour
drum

la guitare électrique
electric guitar

la batterie
drum kit

les styles de musique • musical styles

le jazz
jazz

le blues
blues

la musique punk
punk

la musique folk
folk music

la pop
pop

la danse
dance

le rap
rap

la heavy métal
heavy metal

la musique classique
classical music

---

vocabulaire • vocabulary

la chanson	**les paroles**	**la mélodie**	**le beat**	**le reggae**	**la country**	**le projecteur**
song	lyrics	melody	beat	reggae	country	spotlight

---

le tourisme • sightseeing

le touriste
tourist

l'attraction touristique | tourist attraction

l'itinéraire
itinerary

à impériale
open-top

le bus touristique | tour bus

la guide
tour guide

la visite guidée
guided tour

la statuette
figurine

les souvenirs
souvenirs

vocabulaire • vocabulary

ouvert open	**le guide** guidebook	**le caméscope** camcorder	**à gauche** left	**Où est…?** Where is…?
fermé closed	**la pellicule** film	**l'appareil photo** camera	**à droite** right	**Je me suis perdu.** I'm lost.
le prix d'entrée admission charge	**les piles** batteries	**les directions** directions	**tout droit** straight ahead	**Pour aller à…, s'il vous plaît?** Can you tell me the way to….?

les attractions • attractions

le tableau
painting

l'objet exposé
exhibit

le musée d'art
art gallery

le monument
monument

l'exposition
exhibition

le musée
museum

la ruine célèbre
famous ruin

le monument
historique
historic building

le casino
casino

le parc
gardens

le parc national
national park

l'information • information

les heures
times

le plan
floor plan

le plan
map

l'horaire
schedule

l'information
touristique
tourist information

les activités de plein air • outdoor activities

le sentier
footpath

le cadran solaire
sundial

le café
café

le parc | park

la pelouse
grass

le banc
bench

les jardins à la
française
formal gardens

les montagnes
russes
roller coaster

la foire
fairground

le parc d'attractions
theme park

la réserve
safari park

le zoo
zoo

les activités • activites

le vélo
cycling

le jogging
jogging

la planche à roulette
skateboarding

le roller
rollerblading

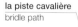

la piste cavalière
bridle path

l'observation des oiseaux
bird-watching

l'équitation
horseback riding

la randonnée
hiking

le panier à pique-nique
hamper

le pique-nique
picnic

le terrain de jeux • playground

le bac à sable
sandbox

la pataugeoire
wading pool

la balançoire
swing

la bascule | seesaw

le toboggan
slide

la cage à poules
climbing frame

la plage • beach

l'hôtel
hotel

le parasol
beach umbrella

la cabine de plage
beach hut

le sable
sand

la vague
wave

la mer
sea

le sac de plage
beach bag

le bikini
bikini

prendre un bain de soleil | sunbathe (v)

le maître nageur
lifeguard

la tour de surveillance
lifeguard tower

le pare-vent
windbreak

la promenade
boardwalk

le transat
deck chair

les lunettes de soleil
sunglasses

le chapeau de plage
sun hat

la lotion solaire
suntan lotion

l'écran total
sunblock

le ballon de plage
beach ball

la bouée
inflatable ring

le maillot de bain
swimsuit

la pelle
shovel

le seau
pail

le château de sable
sandcastle

le coquillage
shell

la serviette de plage
beach towel

le camping • camping

les toilettes
restrooms

les poubelles
waste disposal

les douches
shower block

le branchement électrique
electric hookup

le double toit
flysheet

le piquet
tent peg

la corde
guy rope

la caravane
camper

le terrain de camping
campground

---

vocabulaire • vocabulary

camper camp (v)	**l'emplacement** site	**le banc à pique-nique** picnic bench	**le charbon de bois** charcoal
le bureau du chef site manager's office	**monter une tente** pitch a tent (v)	**le hamac** hammock	**l'allume-feu** firelighter
les emplacements libres sites available	**le mât** tent pole	**le camping-car** camper van	**allumer un feu** light a fire (v)
complet full	**le lit de camp** camp bed	**la remorque** trailer	**le feu de camp** campfire

---

le cadre
frame

le tapis de sol
groundsheet

le sac à dos
backpack

le thermos
vacuum flask

la bouteille d'eau
water bottle

la tente
tent

le spray contre les
insects
insect repellent

la lampe torche
flashlight

la moustiquaire
mosquito net

les sous-vêtements
thermiques
thermal underwear

les chaussures de
marche
hiking boots

l'imperméable
rain gear

le sac de couchage
sleeping bag

le tapis de sol
sleeping mat

le réchaud
camping stove

le barbecue
barbecue grill

le matelat pneumatique | air mattress

les distractions à la maison • home entertainment

le DVD
DVD disk

le lecteur DVD
DVD player

la radio numérique
digital radio

l'iPod®
iPod®

le tourne-disque
record player

le lecteur CD
CD player

la radio
radio

l'amplificateur
amplifier

les écouteurs
headphones

l'étagère
stand

le baffle
(loud) speaker

le support
speaker stand

la chaîne hi-fi
stereo system

l'écran
screen

l'œilleton
eyecup

le box
DTV converter box

le caméscope
camcorder

l'antenne parabolique
satellite dish

la télévision à
écran plat
flatscreen TV

la console
console

l'avance rapide
fast-forward

la pause
pause

l'enregistrement
record

le volume
volume

le retour rapide
rewind

l'arrêt
stop

la commande
controller

la lecture
play

le jeu vidéo | video game

la télécommande
remote control

vocabulaire • vocabulary

le CD CD	**la publicité** advertisement	**le wifi** wifi	**la chaîne à péage** pay-per-view channel	**regarder la télévision** watch television (v)
la cassette cassette tape	**numérique** digital	**le programme** program	**changer de chaîne** change channels (v)	**éteindre la télévision** turn off the television (v)
le lecteur cassettes cassette player	**le streaming** streaming	**stéréo** stereo	**allumer la télévision** turn on the television (v)	**régler la radio** tune the radio (v)
le film feature film	**haute définition** high-definition	**la télévision par câble** cable television		

la photographie • photography

le déclencheur
shutter release

le réglage de l'ouverture
aperture dial

l'objectif
lens

l'appareil réflex mono-objectif | SLR camera

le filtre
filter

le bouchon d'objectif
lens cap

le flash compact
flash gun

le posemètre
light meter

le zoom
zoom lens

le trépied
tripod

les types d'appareils photo • types of camera

le flash
flash

le Polaroid®
Polaroid camera

l'appareil photo APS
APS camera

le photophone
cameraphone

l'appareil jetable
disposable camera

photographier • photograph (v)

le rouleau
de pellicule
film roll

la pellicule
film

mettre au point
focus (v)

développer
develop (v)

le négatif
negative

paysage
landscape

portrait
portrait

la photo | photograph

l'album de photos
photo album

le cadre de photo
picture frame

les problèmes • problems

sous-exposé
underexposed

surexposé
overexposed

flou
out of focus

la tache rouge
red eye

vocabulaire • vocabulary

le viseur
viewfinder

l'épreuve
print

le sac d'appareil photo
camera case

mat
mat

la pose
exposure

brilliant
gloss

la chambre noire
darkroom

l'agrandissement
enlargement

Pourriez-vous faire développer cette pellicule?
I'd like this film processed.

les jeux • games

l'échiquier
chessboard

noir
black

blanc
white

la dame
queen

le roi
king

le fou
bishop

le pion
pawn

la tour
rook

le cavalier
knight

les échecs
chess

la case
square

le pion
piece

la pièce
tile

les dames
checkers

le scrabble
Scrabble

le dé
dice

le jeton
counter

le monopoly
Monopoly

le trictrac | backgammon

les jeux de société | board games

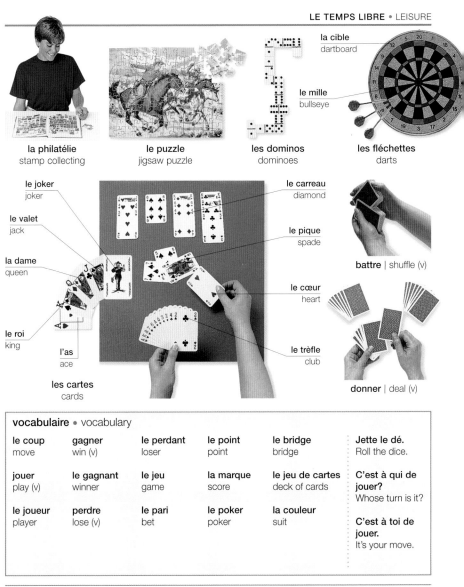

la cible
dartboard

le mille
bullseye

la philatélie
stamp collecting

le puzzle
jigsaw puzzle

les dominos
dominoes

les fléchettes
darts

le joker
joker

le carreau
diamond

le valet
jack

le pique
spade

la dame
queen

battre | shuffle (v)

le roi
king

le cœur
heart

l'as
ace

le trèfle
club

les cartes
cards

donner | deal (v)

---

vocabulaire • vocabulary

le coup move	**gagner** win (v)	**le perdant** loser	**le point** point	**le bridge** bridge	**Jette le dé.** Roll the dice.
jouer play (v)	**le gagnant** winner	**le jeu** game	**la marque** score	**le jeu de cartes** deck of cards	**C'est à qui de jouer?** Whose turn is it?
le joueur player	**perdre** lose (v)	**le pari** bet	**le poker** poker	**la couleur** suit	**C'est à toi de jouer.** It's your move.

---

les arts et métiers 1 • arts and crafts 1

l'artiste peintre
artist

le tableau
painting

le chevalet
easel

la toile
canvas

le pinceau
brush

la palette
palette

la peinture | painting

les couleurs • colours

rouge
red

bleu
blue

jaune
yellow

vert
green

orange
orange

violet
purple

blanc
white

noir
black

gris
gray

rose
pink

marron
brown

indigo
indigo

les couleurs • paints

les peintures à l'huile
oil paints

l'aquarelle
watercolor paint

les pastels
pastels

l'acrylique
acrylic paint

la gouache
poster paint

les autres arts • other crafts

le carnet à croquis
sketchpad

le croquis
sketch

l'encre
ink

le crayon
pencil

le fusain
charcoal

le dessin | drawing

l'imprimerie
printing

la gravure
engraving

la pierre
stone

le maillet
mallet

le burin
chisel

le bois
wood

la spatule
modeling tool

le tour de potier
potter's wheel

la sculpture
sculpting

la sculpture sur bois
woodworking

le carton
cardboard

la colle
glue

l'argile
clay

le collage | collage

la poterie
pottery

la joaillerie
jewelry-making

le papier mâché
papier-mâché

l'origami
origami

le modélisme
model-making

les arts et métiers 2 • arts and crafts 2

le guide de fil
thread guide

la bobine de fil
thread reel

l'aiguille
needle

le balancier
balance wheel

le pied-de-biche
presser foot

la platine
needle plate

le sélecteur de point
stitch selector

la machine à coudre | sewing machine

les ciseaux
scissors

le patron
pattern

la pelote à épingles
pincushion

le centimètre
tape measure

le tissu
material

l'épingle
pin

la corbeille à couture | sewing basket

le fil
thread

l'œillet
eye

la bobine
bobbin

l'agrafe
hook

le dé à coudre
thimble

la craie de tailleur
tailor's chalk

le mannequin
tailor's dummy

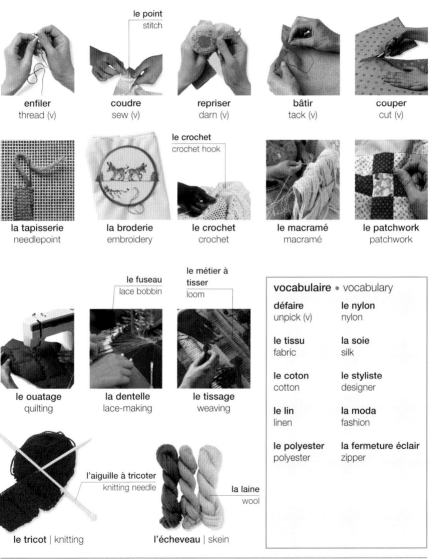

enfiler
thread (v)

le point
stitch

coudre
sew (v)

repriser
darn (v)

bâtir
tack (v)

couper
cut (v)

la tapisserie
needlepoint

la broderie
embroidery

le crochet
crochet hook

le crochet
crochet

le macramé
macramé

le patchwork
patchwork

le métier à
tisser
loom

le fuseau
lace bobbin

le ouatage
quilting

la dentelle
lace-making

le tissage
weaving

vocabulaire • vocabulary

défaire
unpick (v)

le nylon
nylon

le tissu
fabric

la soie
silk

le coton
cotton

le styliste
designer

le lin
linen

la moda
fashion

le polyester
polyester

la fermeture éclair
zipper

l'aiguille à tricoter
knitting needle

la laine
wool

le tricot | knitting

l'écheveau | skein

l'environnement
environment

l'espace • space

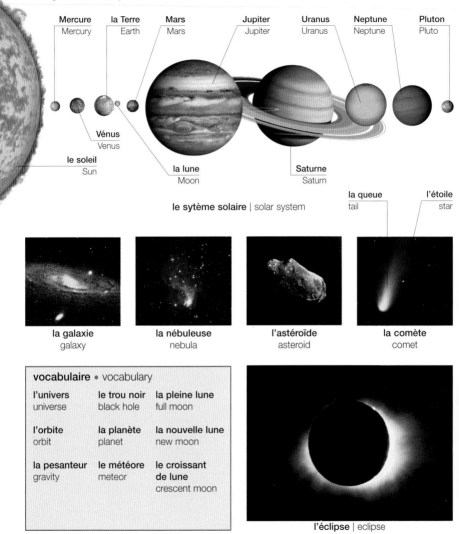

Mercure	la Terre	Mars	Jupiter	Uranus	Neptune	Pluton
Mercury	Earth	Mars	Jupiter	Uranus	Neptune	Pluto

Vénus
Venus

le soleil
Sun

la lune
Moon

Saturne
Saturn

le sytème solaire | solar system

la queue
tail

l'étoile
star

la galaxie
galaxy

la nébuleuse
nebula

l'astéroïde
asteroid

la comète
comet

vocabulaire • vocabulary

l'univers	le trou noir	la pleine lune
universe	black hole	full moon
l'orbite	la planète	la nouvelle lune
orbit	planet	new moon
la pesanteur	le météore	le croissant de lune
gravity	meteor	crescent moon

l'éclipse | eclipse

l'exploration spatiale • space exploration

le radar
radar

la navette spatiale
space shuttle

la fusée d'orientation
thruster

le sas d'équipage
crew hatch

le scaphandre spatial
space suit

l'accélérateur
booster

l'astronaute | astronaut

le module lunaire | lunar module

la rampe de lancement
launch pad

le lancement
launch

le satellite
satellite

la station spatiale
space station

l'astronomie • astronomy

la constellation
constellation

les jumelles
binoculars

le télescope
telescope

le trépied
tripod

la terre • Earth

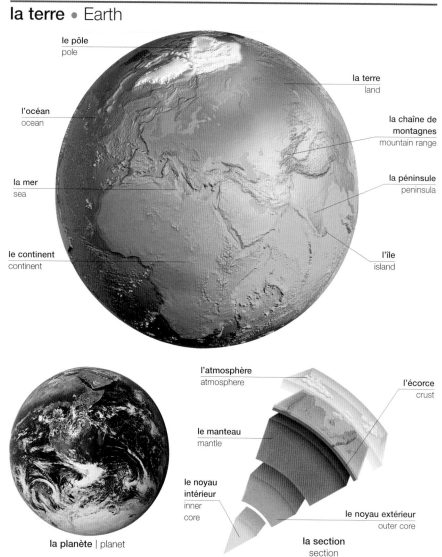

le pôle
pole

la terre
land

l'océan
ocean

la chaîne de
montagnes
mountain range

la mer
sea

la péninsule
peninsula

le continent
continent

l'île
island

l'atmosphère
atmosphere

l'écorce
crust

le manteau
mantle

le noyau
intérieur
inner
core

le noyau extérieur
outer core

la planète | planet

la section
section

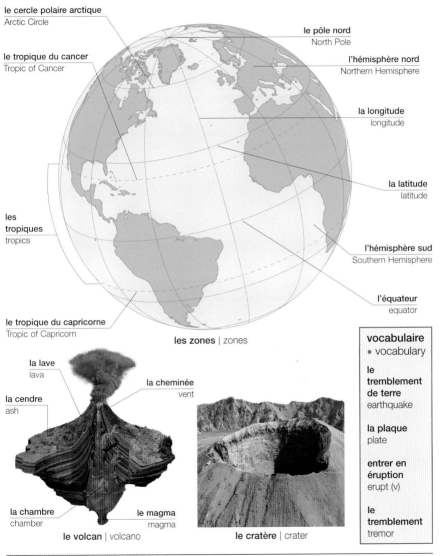

le cercle polaire arctique
Arctic Circle

le tropique du cancer
Tropic of Cancer

les tropiques
tropics

le tropique du capricorne
Tropic of Capricorn

le pôle nord
North Pole

l'hémisphère nord
Northern Hemisphere

la longitude
longitude

la latitude
latitude

l'hémisphère sud
Southern Hemisphere

l'équateur
equator

les zones | zones

la lave
lava

la cheminée
vent

la cendre
ash

la chambre
chamber

le magma
magma

le volcan | volcano

le cratère | crater

vocabulaire
• vocabulary

le tremblement de terre
earthquake

la plaque
plate

entrer en éruption
erupt (v)

le tremblement
tremor

le paysage • landscape

la montagne
mountain

la pente
slope

la rive
bank

la rivière
river

les rapides
rapids

les rochers
rocks

le glacier
glacier

la vallée | valley

la colline
hill

le plateau
plateau

la gorge
gorge

la caverne
cave

la plaine | plain

le désert | desert

la forêt | forest

le bois | woods

la forêt tropicale
rainforest

le marais
swamp

le pré
meadow

la prairie
grassland

la cascade
waterfall

le ruisseau
stream

le lac
lake

le geyser
geyser

la côte
coast

la falaise
cliff

le récif de corail
coral reef

l'estuaire
estuary

le temps • weather

l'exosphère
exosphere

l'aurore
aurora

la thermosphère
thermosphere

l'ionosphère
ionosphere

la mésosphère
mesosphere

les rayons
ultraviolets
ultraviolet rays

la stratosphère
stratosphere

la couche d'ozone
ozone layer

la troposphère
troposphere

l'atmosphère | atmosphere

le soleil
sunshine

le vent
wind

vocabulaire • vocabulary

la neige fondue sleet	**l'averse** shower	**(très) chaud** hot	**sec** dry	**venteux** windy	**J'ai chaud/froid.** I'm hot/cold.
la grêle hail	**ensoleillé** sunny	**froid** cold	**humide** wet	**la tempête** gale	**Il pleut.** It's raining.
le tonnerre thunder	**nuageux** cloudy	**chaud** warm	**lourd** humid	**la température** temperature	**Il fait ... degrés.** It's ... degrees.

l'éclair
lightning

le nuage
cloud

la pluie
rain

l'orage
storm

la brume
mist

le brouillard
fog

l'arc-en-ciel
rainbow

le glaçon
icicle

la neige
snow

le givre
frost

la glace
ice

le gel
freeze

l'ouragan
hurricane

la tornade
tornado

la mousson
monsoon

l'inondation
flood

les roches • rocks

igné • igneous

le granit
granite

l'obsidienne
obsidian

le basalte
basalt

la pierre ponce
pumice

sédimentaire • sedimentary

le grès
sandstone

le calcaire
limestone

la craie
chalk

le silex
flint

le conglomérat
conglomerate

le charbon
coal

métamorphique • metamorphic

l'ardoise
slate

le schiste
schist

le gneiss
gneiss

le marbre
marble

les gemmes • gems

le rubis
ruby

l'aigue-marine
aquamarine

l'améthyste
amethyst

le diamant
diamond

le jade
jade

le jais
jet

l'émeraude
emerald

l'opale
opal

le saphir
sapphire

la pierre de lune
moonstone

le grenat
garnet

le topaze
topaz

la toumaline
tourmaline

les minéraux • minerals

le quartz
quartz

le mica
mica

le soufre
sulfur

l'hématite
hematite

la calcite
calcite

la malachite
malachite

la turquoise
turquoise

l'onyx
onyx

l'agate
agate

le graphite
graphite

les métaux • metals

l'or
gold

l'argent
silver

le platine
platinum

le nickel
nickel

le fer
iron

le cuivre
copper

l'étain
tin

l'aluminium
aluminum

le mercure
mercury

le zinc
zinc

les animaux 1 • animals 1
les mammifères • mammals

les poils
whiskers

la queue
tail

le lapin
rabbit

le hamster
hamster

la souris
mouse

le rat
rat

le hérisson
hedgehog

l'écureuil
squirrel

la chauve-souris
bat

le raton laveur
raccoon

le renard
fox

le loup
wolf

le chiot
puppy

le chaton
kitten

le bébé-phoque
pup

le chien
dog

le chat
cat

la loutre
otter

le phoque
seal

la nageoire
flipper

l'évent
blowhole

l'otarie
sea lion

le morse
walrus

la baleine
whale

le dauphin
dolphin

la ramure
antler

le cerf
deer

la crinière
mane

le sabot
hoof

le zèbre
zebra

la girafe
giraffe

la bosse
hump

le chameau
camel

l'hippopotame
hippopotamus

la trompe
trunk

la défense
tusk

l'éléphant
elephant

la corne
horn

le rhinocéros
rhinoceros

le tigre
tiger

la crinière
mane

le lion
lion

le singe
monkey

le gorille
gorilla

le koala
koala

la poche
pouch

le kangourou
kangaroo

l'ours
bear

la griffe
claw

l'ours blanc
polar bear

le panda
panda

français • english

les animaux 2 • animals 2

les oiseaux • birds

la queue
tail

le canari
canary

le moineau
sparrow

le colibri
hummingbird

l'hirondelle
swallow

le corbeau
crow

le pigeon
pigeon

le pic
woodpecker

le faucon
falcon

la chouette
owl

la mouette
gull

l'aigle
eagle

le pélican
pelican

le flamant
flamingo

la cigogne
stork

la grue
crane

le pingouin
penguin

l'autruche
ostrich

les reptiles • reptiles

l'oie | goose

le cygne
swan

le paon
peacock

le faisan
pheasant

le dindon
turkey

le cacatoès
cockatoo

le bec
beak

la plume
feather

l'aile
wing

la griffe
claw

le perroquet
parrot

les écailles
scales

l'alligator
alligator

le lézard
lizard

l'iguane
iguana

la carapace
shell

la tortue marine
turtle

la tortue
tortoise

le serpent
snake

le museau
snout

le crocodile
crocodile

les animaux 3 • animals 3
les amphibiens • amphibians

la grenouille
frog

le crapaud
toad

le têtard
tadpole

la salamandre
salamander

les poissons • fish

l'anguille
eel

le requin
shark

l'hippocampe
sea horse

la raie
skate

la raie
ray

le poisson rouge
goldfish

la nageoire dorsale
dorsal fin

la nageoire pectorale
pectoral fin

la queue
tail

l'écaille
scale

l'ouïe
gill

l'espadon
swordfish

la carpe koi
koi carp

es invertébrés • invertebrates

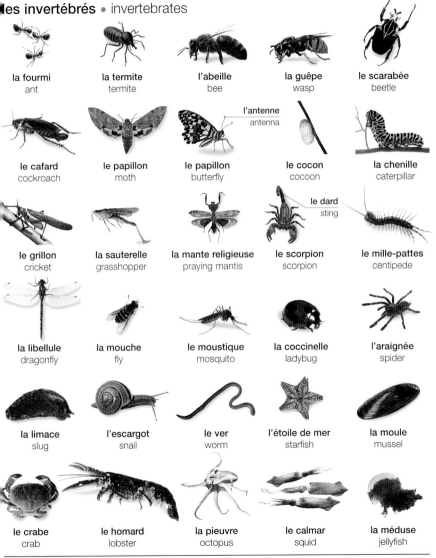

la fourmi
ant

la termite
termite

l'abeille
bee

la guêpe
wasp

le scarabée
beetle

le cafard
cockroach

le papillon
moth

le papillon
butterfly

l'antenne
antenna

le cocon
cocoon

la chenille
caterpillar

le grillon
cricket

la sauterelle
grasshopper

la mante religieuse
praying mantis

le dard
sting

le scorpion
scorpion

le mille-pattes
centipede

la libellule
dragonfly

la mouche
fly

le moustique
mosquito

la coccinelle
ladybug

l'araignée
spider

la limace
slug

l'escargot
snail

le ver
worm

l'étoile de mer
starfish

la moule
mussel

le crabe
crab

le homard
lobster

la pieuvre
octopus

le calmar
squid

la méduse
jellyfish

les plantes • plants

l'arbre • tree

la feuille
leaf

la branche
branch

la brindille
twig

l'écorce
bark

le saule
willow

la racine
root

le tronc
trunk

le chêne
oak

le peuplier
poplar

l'eucalyptus
eucalyptus

le mélèze
larch

le hêtre
beech

le bouleau
birch

le pin
pine

le cèdre
cedar

l'érable
maple

l'orme
elm

le tilleul
lime

le houx
holly

la baie
berry

le palmier
palm

la plante à fleurs • flowering plant

la fleur
flower

l'étamine
stamen

le pétale
petal

le calice
calyx

la tige
stalk

la tige
stem

le bouton
bud

la renoncule
buttercup

la pâquerette
daisy

le chardon
thistle

le pissenlit
dandelion

la bruyère
heather

le coquelicot
poppy

la digitale
foxglove

le chèvrefeuille
honeysuckle

le tournesol
sunflower

le trèfle
clover

les jacinthes
des bois
bluebells

la primevère
primrose

les lupins
lupines

l'ortie
nettle

la ville • town

la rue
street

le bord du trottoir
curb

le coin de la rue
street corner

le magasin
store

le carrefour
intersection

la voie à
sens unique
one-way
system

le trottoir
sidewalk

l'immeuble
de bureaux
office
building

l'immeuble
apartment
building

la ruelle
alley

le parking
parking lot

le panneau de signalisation
street sign

la borne
barrier

le lampadaire
streetlight

les bâtiments • buildings

la mairie
town hall

la bibliothèque
library

le cinéma
movie theater

le théâtre
theater

l'université
university

les environs • areas

la zone industrielle
industrial park

la ville
city

l'école
school

le gratte-ciel
skyscraper

la banlieue
suburb

le village
village

---

vocabulaire • vocabulary

la zone piétonnière pedestrian zone	**la rue transversale** side street	**la bouche d'égout** manhole	**le caniveau** gutter	**l'église** church
l'avenue avenue	**la place** square	**l'arrêt de bus** bus stop	**l'usine** factory	**l'égout** drain

---

l'architecture • architecture

les bâtiments et structures • buildings and structures

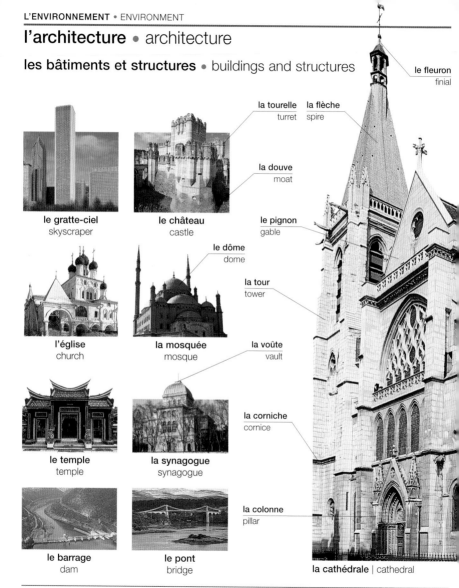

le fleuron
finial

la tourelle
turret

la flèche
spire

la douve
moat

le gratte-ciel
skyscraper

le château
castle

le pignon
gable

le dôme
dome

la tour
tower

l'église
church

la mosquée
mosque

la voûte
vault

la corniche
cornice

le temple
temple

la synagogue
synagogue

la colonne
pillar

le barrage
dam

le pont
bridge

la cathédrale | cathedral

les styles • styles

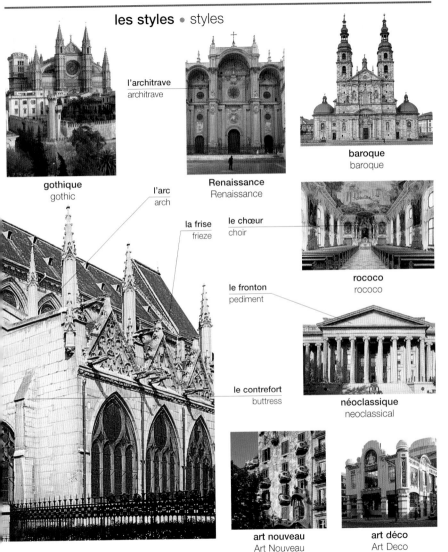

gothique
gothic

l'architrave
architrave

Renaissance
Renaissance

baroque
baroque

l'arc
arch

la frise
frieze

le chœur
choir

rococo
rococo

le fronton
pediment

le contrefort
buttress

néoclassique
neoclassical

art nouveau
Art Nouveau

art déco
Art Deco

l'information
reference

l'heure • time

la grande aiguille
minute hand

la petite aiguille
hour hand

l'horloge
clock

vocabulaire • vocabulary

la seconde second	**maintenant** now	**un quart d'heure** 15 minutes
la minute minute	**plus tard** later	**vingt minutes** twenty minutes
l'heure hour	**une demi-heure** half an hour	**quarante minutes** forty minutes

Quelle heure est-il?
What time is it?

Il est trois heures.
It's three o'clock.

une heure cinq
five after one

une heure dix
ten after one

une heure et quart
quarter after one

une heure vingt
twenty after one

la trotteuse
second hand

une heure vingt-cinq
twenty-five after one

une heure trente
one-thirty

deux heures moins vingt-cinq
twenty-five to two

deux heures moins vingt
twenty to two

deux heures moins le quart
quarter to two

deux heures moins dix
ten to two

deux heures moins cinq
five to two

deux heures
two o'clock

la nuit et le jour • night and day

minuit
midnight

le lever du soleil
sunrise

l'aube
dawn

le matin
morning

le coucher du soleil
sunset

(le) midi
noon

le crépuscule
dusk

le soir
evening

l'après-midi
afternoon

---

vocabulaire • vocabulary

tôt early	**Tu es en avance.** You're early.	**Sois à l'heure, s'il te plaît.** Please be on time.	**Ça finit à quelle heure?** What time does it end?
à l'heure on time	**Tu es en retard.** You're late.	**À tout à l'heure.** I'll see you later.	**Il se fait tard.** It's getting late.
tard late	**J'y arriverai bientôt.** I'll be there soon.	**Ça commence à quelle heure?** What time does it start?	**Ça dure combien de temps?** How long will it last?

le calendrier • calendar

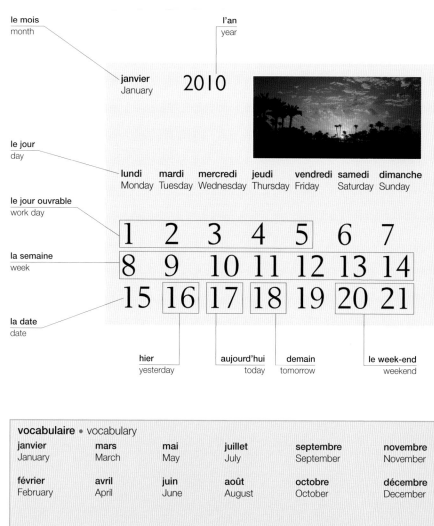

le mois
month

l'an
year

janvier
January

2010

le jour
day

lundi **mardi** **mercredi** **jeudi** **vendredi** **samedi** **dimanche**
Monday Tuesday Wednesday Thursday Friday Saturday Sunday

le jour ouvrable
work day

1 2 3 4 5 6 7

la semaine
week

8 9 10 11 12 13 14

15 16 17 18 19 20 21

la date
date

hier
yesterday

aujourd'hui
today

demain
tomorrow

le week-end
weekend

vocabulaire • vocabulary

janvier January	**mars** March	**mai** May	**juillet** July	**septembre** September	**novembre** November
février February	**avril** April	**juin** June	**août** August	**octobre** October	**décembre** December

les ans • years

1900   **mille neuf cents** • nineteen hundred

1901   **mille neuf cent un** • nineteen hundred and one

1910   **mille neuf cent dix** • nineteen ten

2000   **deux mille** • two thousand

2001   **deux mille un** • two thousand and one

les saisons • seasons

le printemps
spring

l'été
summer

l'automne
fall

l'hiver
winter

---

vocabulaire • vocabulary

le siècle century	**la semaine dernière** last week	**mensuel** monthly
la décennie decade	**la semaine prochaine** next week	**annuel** annual
le millénaire millennium	**avant-hier** the day before yesterday	
cette semaine this week	**après-demain** the day after tomorrow	**Quelle est la date aujourd'hui?** What's the date today?
	hebdomadaire weekly	**C'est le sept février deux mille deux.** It's February seventh, two thousand and two.

les nombres • numbers

0	**zéro** • zero		20	**vingt** • twenty
1	**un** • one		21	**vingt et un** • twenty-one
2	**deux** • two		22	**vingt-deux** • twenty-two
3	**trois** • three		30	**trente** • thirty
4	**quatre** • four		40	**quarante** • forty
5	**cinq** • five		50	**cinquante** • fifty
6	**six** • six		60	**soixante** • sixty
7	**sept** • seven		70	**soixante-dix** • seventy
8	**huit** • eight		80	**quatre-vingts** • eighty
9	**neuf** • nine		90	**quatre-vingt-dix** • ninety
10	**dix** • ten		100	**cent** • one hundred
11	**onze** • eleven		110	**cent dix** • one hundred and ten
12	**douze** • twelve		200	**deux cents** • two hundred
13	**treize** • thirteen		300	**trois cents** • three hundred
14	**quatorze** • fourteen		400	**quatre cents** • four hundred
15	**quinze** • fifteen		500	**cinq cents** • five hundred
16	**seize** • sixteen		600	**six cents** • six hundred
17	**dix-sept** • seventeen		700	**sept cents** • seven hundred
18	**dix-huit** • eighteen		800	**huit cents** • eight hundred
19	**dix-neuf** • nineteen		900	**neuf cents** • nine hundred

1,000   **mille** • one thousand

10,000   **dix mille** • ten thousand

20,000   **vingt mille** • twenty thousand

50,000   **cinquante mille** • fifty thousand

55,500   **cinqante-cinq mille cinq cents** • fifty-five thousand five hundred

100,000   **cent mille** • one hundred thousand

1,000,000   **un million** • one million

1,000,000,000   **un milliard** • one billion

premier / first
deuxième / second
troisième / third

quatrième • fourth

cinquième • fifth

sixième • sixth

septième • seventh

huitième • eighth

neuvième • ninth

dixième • tenth

onzième • eleventh

douzième • twelfth

treizième • thirteenth

quatorzième • fourteenth

quinzième • fifteenth

seizième
• sixteenth

dix-septième
• seventeenth

dix-huitième
• eighteenth

dix-neuvième
• nineteenth

vingtième
• twentieth

vingt et unième
• twenty-first

vingt-deuxième
• twenty-second

vingt-troisième
• twenty-third

trentième • thirtieth

quarantième • fortieth

cinquantième • fiftieth

soixantième • sixtieth

soixante-dixième
• seventieth

quatre-vingtième
• eightieth

quatre-vingt-dixième
• ninetieth

centième
• one hundredth

français • english

les poids et mesures • weights and measures

la superficie • area

le pied carré
square foot

le mètre carré
square meter

la distance • distance

le kilomètre
kilometer

le mile
mile

le plateau
pan

la livre
pound

l'once
ounce

le kilogramme
kilogram

le gramme
gram

la balance | scale

vocabulaire • vocabulary		
le yard yard	**la tonne** ton	**mesurer** measure (v)
le mètre meter	**le milligramme** milligram	**peser** weigh (v)

la longueur • length

le pied
foot

le millimètre
millimeter

le centimètre
centimeter

le pouce
inch

la capacité • capacity

le demi-litre
half-liter

la pinte
pint

le volume
volume

le millilitre
milliliter

le verre mesureur
measuring cup

la mesure pour les liquides
liquid measure

vocabulaire • vocabulary

le gallon
gallon

deux pintes
quart

le litre
liter

le récipient • container

la brique
carton

le paquet
packet

la bouteille
bottle

le sac
bag

le pot | tub

le pot | jar

la boîte
can

la boîte | tin

le pulvérisateur
spray bottle

le pain
bar

le tube
tube

le rouleau
roll

le paquet
pack

la bombe
spray can

la carte du monde • world map

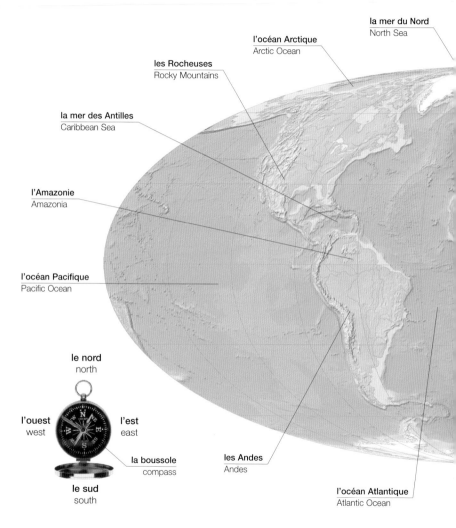

la mer du Nord
North Sea

l'océan Arctique
Arctic Ocean

les Rocheuses
Rocky Mountains

la mer des Antilles
Caribbean Sea

l'Amazonie
Amazonia

l'océan Pacifique
Pacific Ocean

le nord
north

l'ouest
west

l'est
east

la boussole
compass

le sud
south

les Andes
Andes

l'océan Atlantique
Atlantic Ocean

la mer Baltique
Baltic Sea

la Méditerranée
Mediterranean Sea

la Sibérie
Siberia

la mer Noire
Black Sea

la mer Caspienne
Caspian Sea

l'Himalaya
Himalayas

la mer d'Arabie
Arabian Sea

l'océan Indien
Indian Ocean

la mer Rouge
Red Sea

le Sahara
Sahara Desert

l'océan Austral
Southern Ocean

français • english

l'Amérique du Nord et centrale • North and Central America

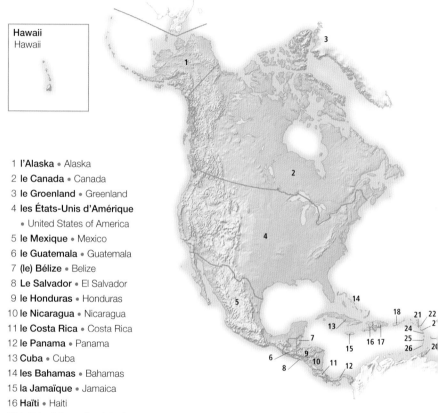

Hawaii
Hawaii

1 l'Alaska • Alaska
2 le Canada • Canada
3 le Groenland • Greenland
4 les États-Unis d'Amérique
  • United States of America
5 le Mexique • Mexico
6 le Guatemala • Guatemala
7 (le) Bélize • Belize
8 Le Salvador • El Salvador
9 le Honduras • Honduras
10 le Nicaragua • Nicaragua
11 le Costa Rica • Costa Rica
12 le Panama • Panama
13 Cuba • Cuba
14 les Bahamas • Bahamas
15 la Jamaïque • Jamaica
16 Haïti • Haiti
17 la République dominicaine
  • Dominican Republic
18 la Porto Rico • Puerto Rico
19 la Barbade • Barbados
20 la Trinité-et-Tobago • Trinidad and Tobago
21 Saint-Kitts-et-Nevis • St. Kitts and Nevis

22 Antigua-et-Barbuda • Antigua and Barbuda
23 la Dominique • Dominica
24 Sainte-Lucie • St. Lucia
25 Saint-Vincent-et-les-Grenadines
  • St. Vincent and The Grenadines
26 la Grenade • Grenada

l'Amérique du Sud • South America

1 **le Venezuela** • Venezuela
2 **la Colombie** • Colombia
3 **l'Équateur** • Ecuador
4 **le Pérou** • Peru
5 **les îles Galapagos**
  • Galapagos Islands
6 **la Guyane** • Guyana
7 **le Surinam** • Suriname
8 **la Guyane française**
  • French Guiana
9 **le Brésil** • Brazil
10 **la Bolivie** • Bolivia
11 **le Chili** • Chile
12 **l'Argentine** • Argentina
13 **le Paraguay** • Paraguay
14 **l'Uruguay** • Uruguay
15 **les îles Malouines**
  • Falkland Islands

vocabulaire • vocabulary		
le pays country	**la province** province	**la zone** zone
la nation nation	**le territoire** territory	**le district** district
l'État state	**la colonie** colony	**la région** region
le continent continent	**la principauté** principality	**la capitale** capital

l'Europe • Europe

1 l'Irlande • Ireland

2 le Royaume-Uni • United Kingdom

3 le Portugal • Portugal

4 l'Espagne • Spain

5 les Baléares • Balearic Islands

6 l'Andorre • Andorra

7 la France • France

8 la Belgique • Belgium

9 les Pays-Bas • Netherlands

10 le Luxembourg
• Luxembourg

11 l'Allemagne • Germany

12 le Danemark • Denmark

13 la Norvège • Norway

14 la Suède • Sweden

15 la Finlande • Finland

16 l'Estonie • Estonia

17 la Lettonie • Latvia

18 la Lituanie • Lithuania

19 Kaliningrad • Kaliningrad

20 la Pologne • Poland

21 la République tchèque
• Czech Republic

22 l'Autriche • Austria

23 le Liechtenstein
• Liechtenstein

24 la Suisse
• Switzerland

25 l'Italie • Italy

26 Monaco
• Monaco

27 la Corse
• Corsica

28 la Sardaigne
• Sardinia

29 le Saint-Marin • San Marino

30 la Cité du Vatican
• Vatican City

31 la Sicile • Sicily

32 Malte • Malta

33 la Slovénie • Slovenia

34 la Croatie • Croatia

35 la Hongrie • Hungary

36 la Slovaquie • Slovakia

37 l'Ukraine • Ukraine

38 la Bélarus • Belarus

39 la Moldavie • Moldova

40 la Roumanie • Romania

41 la Serbie • Serbia

42 la Bosnie-Herzégovine
• Bosnia and Herzogovina

43 l'Albanie • Albania

44 la Macédonie • Macedonia

45 la Bulgarie • Bulgaria

46 la Grèce • Greece

47 le Kosovo • Kosovo

48 Montenegro • Montenegro

49 l'Islande • Iceland

l'Afrique • Africa

1 le Maroc • Morocco
2 le Sahara occidental
  • Western Sahara
3 la Mauritanie
  • Mauritania
4 le Sénégal • Senegal
5 la Gambie • Gambia
6 la Guinée-Bissau
  • Guinea-Bissau
7 la Guinée • Guinea
8 la Sierra Leone
  • Sierra Leone
9 le Libéria • Liberia
10 la Côte d'Ivoire
  • Ivory Coast
11 le Burkina • Burkina Faso
12 le Mali • Mali
13 l'Algérie • Algeria
14 la Tunisie • Tunisia
15 la Libye • Libya
16 le Niger • Niger
17 le Ghana • Ghana
18 le Togo • Togo
19 le Bénin • Benin

20 le Nigéria • Nigeria
21 Sao Tomé-et-Principe
  • São Tomé and Principe
22 la Guinée équatoriale
  • Equatorial Guinea
23 le Cameroun • Cameroon
24 le Tchad • Chad
25 l'Égypte • Egypt
26 le Soudan • Sudan
27 le Soudan du Sud
  • South Sudan
28 l'Érythrée • Eritrea
29 Djibouti • Djibouti
30 l'Éthiopie • Ethiopia
31 la Somalie • Somalia

32 le Kenya • Kenya
33 l'Ouganda • Uganda
34 la République centrafricaine
  • Central African Republic
35 le Gabon • Gabon
36 le Congo • Congo
37 Cabinda • Cabinda
38 la République démocratique
  du Congo • Democratic
  Republic of the Congo
39 le Rwanda • Rwanda
40 le Burundi • Burundi
41 la Tanzanie • Tanzania
42 le Mozambique
  • Mozambique
43 le Malawi • Malawi
44 la Zambie • Zambia
45 l'Angola • Angola
46 la Namibie • Namibia
47 le Botswana • Botswana
48 le Zimbabwe • Zimbabwe
49 l'Afrique du Sud
  • South Africa
50 le Lesotho • Lesotho
51 le Swaziland • Swaziland
52 les Comores • Comoros
53 Madagascar • Madagascar
54 l'île Maurice • Mauritius

français • english

317

l'Asie • Asia

1 **la Turquie** • Turkey

2 **Chypre** • Cyprus

3 **la Fédération de Russie**
• Russian Federation

4 **la Géorgie** • Georgia

5 **l'Arménie** • Armenia

6 **l'Azerbaïdjan** • Azerbaijan

7 **l'Iran** • Iran

8 **l'Irak** • Iraq

9 **la Syrie** • Syria

10 **le Liban** • Lebanon

11 **Israël** • Israel

12 **la Jordanie** • Jordan

13 **l'Arabie Saoudite**
• Saudi Arabia

14 **le Koweït** • Kuwait

15 **Bahreïn** • Bahrain

16 **le Qatar** • Qatar

17 **les Émirats arabes unis**
• United Arab Emirates

18 **l'Oman** • Oman

19 **le Yémen** • Yemen

20 **le Kasakhastan** • Kazakhstan

21 **l'Ouzbékistan** • Uzbekistan

22 **le Turkmenistan** • Turkmenistan

23 **l'Afghanistan** • Afghanistan

24 **le Tadjikistan** • Tajikistan

25 **le Kirghizistan** • Kyrgyzstan

26 **le Pakistan** • Pakistan

27 **l'Inde** • India

28 **les Maldives** • Maldives

29 **Sri Lanka** • Sri Lanka

30 **la Chine** • China

31 **la Mongolie** • Mongolia

32 **la Corée du Nord** • North Korea

33 **la Corée du Sud** • South Korea

34 **le Japon** • Japan

35 **le Népal** • Nepal

36 **le Bhoutan** • Bhutan

37 **le Bangladesh** • Bangladesh

38 **la Birmaniem (le Myanmar)**
• Burma (Myanmar)

39 **la Thaïlande** • Thailand

40 **le Laos** • Laos

41 **le Vietnam** • Vietnam

français • english

l'Australasie • Australasia

1 **l'Australie** • Australia
2 **la Tasmanie** • Tasmania
3 **la Nouvelle-Zélande** • New Zealand

42 **le Cambodge** • Cambodia
43 **la Malaisie** • Malaysia
44 **Singapour** • Singapore
45 **l'Indonésie** • Indonesia
46 **le Brunei** • Brunei
47 **les Philippines** • Philippines
48 **le Timor oriental** • East Timor
49 **la Papouasie-Nouvelle-Guinée**
  • Papua New Guinea
50 **les îles Salomon** • Solomon Islands
51 **Vanuatu** • Vanuatu
52 **Fidji** • Fiji

particules et antonymes • particles and antonyms

à to	**de** from	**pour** for	**vers** toward
au-dessus de over	**sous** under	**le long de** along	**à travers** across
devant in front of	**derrière** behind	**avec** with	**sans** without
sur onto	**dans** into	**avant** before	**après** after
dans in	**dehors** out	**avant** by	**jusqu'à** until
au-dessus de above	**au-dessous de** below	**tôt** early	**tard** late
à l'intérieur de inside	**à l'extérieur de** outside	**maintenant** now	**plus tard** later
en haut up	**en bas** down	**toujours** always	**jamais** never
à at	**au-delà de** beyond	**souvent** often	**rarement** rarely
à travers through	**autour de** around	**hier** yesterday	**demain** tomorrow
sur on top of	**à côté de** beside	**premier** first	**dernier** last
entre between	**en face de** opposite	**chaque** every	**quelque** some
près de near	**loin de** far	**vers** about	**exactement** exactly
ici here	**là** there	**un peu** a little	**beaucoup** a lot

grand large	**petit** small	**chaud** hot	**froid** cold
large wide	**étroit** narrow	**ouvert** open	**fermé** closed
grand tall	**court** short	**plein** full	**vide** empty
haut high	**bas** low	**neuf** new	**vieux** old
épais thick	**mince** thin	**clair** light	**foncé** dark
léger light	**lourd** heavy	**facile** easy	**difficile** difficult
dur hard	**mou** soft	**libre** free	**occupé** occupied
humide wet	**sec** dry	**fort** strong	**faible** weak
bon good	**mauvais** bad	**gros** fat	**mince** thin
rapide fast	**lent** slow	**jeune** young	**vieux** old
juste correct	**faux** wrong	**mieux** better	**pire** worse
propre clean	**sale** dirty	**noir** black	**blanc** white
beau beautiful	**laid** ugly	**intéressant** interesting	**ennuyeux** boring
cher expensive	**bon marché** cheap	**malade** sick	**bien** well
silencieux quiet	**bruyant** noisy	**le début** beginning	**la fin** end

phrases utiles • useful phrases

phrases essentielles
• essential phrases

Oui
Yes

Non
No

Peut-être
Maybe

S'il vous plaît
Please

Merci
Thank you

De rien
You're welcome

Pardon
Excuse me

Je suis désolé
I'm sorry

Ne... pas
Don't

D'accord
OK

Très bien
That's fine

C'est juste
That's correct

C'est faux
That's wrong

salutations
• greetings

Bonjour
Hello

Au revoir
Goodbye

Bonjour
Good morning

Bonjour
Good afternoon

Bonsoir
Good evening

Bonne nuit
Good night

Comment allez-vous?
How are you?

Je m'appelle...
My name is...

Vous vous appelez comment?
What is your name?

Il/Elle s'appelle comment?
What is his/her name?

Je vous présente...
May I introduce...

C'est...
This is...

Enchanté
Pleased to meet you

À tout à l'heure
See you later

panneaux • signs

Office de tourisme
Tourist information

Entrée
Entrance

Sortie
Exit

Sortie de secours
Emergency exit

Poussez
Push

Danger
Danger

Défense de fumer
No smoking

En panne
Out of order

Heures d'ouverture
Opening times

Entrée gratuite
Free admission

Journée continue
Open all day

Prix réduit
Reduced price

Soldes
Sale

Frappez avant d'entrer
Knock before entering

Défense de marcher sur la pelouse
Keep off the grass

assistance • help

Pouvez-vous m'aider?
Can you help me?

Je ne comprends pas
I don't understand

Je ne sais pas
I don't know

Vous parlez anglais, français...?
Do you speak English, French...?

Je parle anglais, espagnol...
I speak English, Spanish...

Parlez moins vite, s'il vous plaît
Please speak more slowly

Écrivez-le pour moi, s'il vous plaît
Please write it down for me

J'ai perdu...
I have lost...

directions
• directions

Je me suis perdu
I am lost

Où est le/la…?
Where is the…?

Où est le/la…le/la plus proche?
Where is the nearest…?

Où sont les toilettes?
Where are the restrooms?

Pour aller à…?
How do I get to…?

À droite
To the right

À gauche
To the left

Tout droit
Straight ahead

C'est loin…?
How far is…?

les panneaux routiers
• road signs

Toutes directions
All directions

Prudence
Caution

Entrée interdite
No entry

Ralentir
Slow down

Déviation
Detour

Serrez à droite
Keep right

Autoroute
Freeway

Stationnement interdit
No parking

Passage interdit
No through road

Sens unique
One-way street

Autres directions
Other directions

Riverains autorisés
Residents only

Travaux
Road construction

Virage dangereux
Dangerous bend

logement •
accommodation

J'ai réservé une chambre
I have a reservation

Où est la salle à manger?
Where is the dining room?

Le numéro de ma chambre est le …
My room number is …

Le petit déjeuner est à quelle heure?
What time is breakfast?

Je serai de retour à … heures
I'll be back at … o'clock

Je pars demain
I'm leaving tomorrow

nourriture et boissons
• eating and drinking

À la vôtre!
Cheers!

C'est délicieux/terrible
It's delicious/awful

Je ne bois/fume pas
I don't drink/smoke

Je ne mange pas de la viande
I don't eat meat

Je n'en veux plus, merci
No more for me, thank you

Encore un peu, s'il vous plaît.
May I have some more?

L'addition, s'il vous plaît.
May we have the bill/check?

Je voudrais un reçu.
Can I have a receipt?

Partie non-fumeurs
No-smoking area

la santé
• health

Je ne me sens pas bien
I don't feel well

J'ai envie de vomir
I feel sick

Pouvez-vous me donner le numéro de téléphone du docteur le plus proche?
What is the telephone number of the nearest doctor?

J'ai mal ici
It hurts here

J'ai de la fièvre
I have a fever

Je suis enceinte de …mois
I'm … months pregnant

J'ai besoin d'une ordonnance pour …
I need a prescription for …

Je prends habituellement …
I normally take …

Je suis allergique à …
I'm allergic to …

index français • French index

français

français

français

français

français

français

français

français • english

français

index anglais • English index

english

english

english

embarrassed 25
embossed paper 83
embroidery 277
embryo 52
emerald 288
emergency 46
emergency exit 210
emergency lever 209
emergency phone 195
emergency room 48
emergency services 94
emigrate v 26
emotions 25
employee 24
employer 24
empty 321
enamel 50
encore 255
encyclopedia 163
end 321
end zone 220
endive 123
endline 226
endocrine 19
endocrinology 49
energy-saving bulb
(eco bulb) 60
engaged couple 24
engine 202, 204, 208,
210
engine room 214
engineering 169
English breakfast 157
English horn 257
English mustard 135
engraving 275
enlarge v 172
enlargement 271
entrance 59
entrance ramp 194
entrée 153
envelope 98, 173
environment 280
epidural 52
epiglottis 19
epilepsy 44
episiotomy 52
equals 165
equation 165
equator 283
equipment 233, 238
equipment 165
Equatorial Guinea 317
equity 97
eraser 163
Eritrea 317
erupt v 283
escalator 104
esophagus 19
espresso 148
essay 163
essential oils 55
estate 199
Estonia 316

estuary 285
Ethiopia 317
eucalyptus 296
Europe 316
evening 305
evening dress 34
events 243, 247
evergreen 86
evidence 181
examination 163
excavator 187
excess baggage 212
exchange rate 97
excited 25
excuse me 322
executive 174
exercise bike 250
exercises 251
exfoliate v 41
exhaust pipe 203, 204
exhibit v 261
exhibition 261
exit 210
exit ramp 194
exosphere 286
expectant 52
experiment 166
expiration date 109
exposure 271
express train 209
extend v 251
extension 58
extension cord 78
exterior 198
external hard drive 176
extra time 223
extraction 50
extractor 66
eye 14, 51, 244, 276
eye shadow 40
eye test 51
eyebrow 14, 51
eyebrow brush 40
eyebrow pencil 40
eyecup 269
eyelash 14, 51
eyelet 37
eyelid 51
eyeliner 40
eyepiece 167

F

fabric 277
fabric conditioner 76
face 14
face cream 73
face mask 225
face pack 41
face powder 40
faceoff circle 224
facial 41
factory 299
faint v 25, 44
fair 41

fairground 262
fairway 232
falcon 292
Falkland Islands 315
fall 237
fall (autumn) 31, 307
fall in love v 26
fallopian tube 20
family 22
famous ruin 261
fan 60, 202
fan belt 203
far 320
fare 197, 209
farm 182, 183, 184
farmer 182, 189
farmhouse 182
farmland 182
farmyard 182
farsightedness 51
fashion 277
fast 321
fast food 154
fast-forward 269
fastening 37
fat 119, 321
fat-free 137
fat-free milk 136
father 22
father-in-law 23
fault 230
fava beans 122, 131
fax 98, 172
fax machine 172
feather 293
feature film 269
February 306
feed v 183
feijoa 128
female 12, 20
feminine hygiene 108
femur 17
fence 85, 182, 243
fencerow 182
fencing 249
feng shui 55
fennel 122, 133
fennel seeds 133
fenugreek 132
fern 86
ferry 215, 216
ferry terminal 216
fertilization 20
fertilize v 91
fertilizer 91
festivals 27
fetus 52
fever 44
fiancé 24
fiancée 24
fiber 127
fibula 17
field 182, 222, 225, 228,
234, 258, 266

field v 225, 229
field hockey 224
fifteen 308
fifteenth 309
fifth 309
fiftieth 309
fifty 308
fifty five thousand, five
hundred 309
fifty thousand 309
fig 129
fighter plane 211
figure skating 247
figurine 260
Fiji 319
filament 60
file 81, 177
filing cabinet 172
fill v 82
filler 83
fillet 119, 121
filleted 121
filling 50, 140, 155
film chamber 270
film roll 271
film set 179
filter 270
filter coffee 148
filter paper 167
fin 210
finance 97
financial advisor 97
fingerprint 94
finial 300
finish line 234
Finland 316
fire 95
fire alarm 95
fire department 95
fire engine 95
fire escape 95
fire extinguisher 95
fire station 95
firefighter 95, 189
firelighter 266
fireplace 63
firm 124
first 309
first aid 47
first-aid box 47
fish 107, 120, 294
fish and chips 155
fish farm 183
fisherman 189
fishhook 244
fishing 244, 245
fishing boat 217
fishing license 245
fishing port 217
fishing rod 244
fishmonger 114, 120,
188
fist 15, 237
fitness 250

five 308
five hundred 308
flag 221, 232
flageolet beans 131
flakes 132
flamingo 292
flan 142
flan tin 69
flare 240
flash 270
flash gun 270
flashlight 267
flask 166
flat 59, 256
flat race 243
flat tire 203, 207
flat wood bit 80
flatbread 139
flatscreen TV 269
flavored oil 134
flax 184
fleece 74
flesh 124, 127, 129
flex v 251
flight attendant 190, 210
flight number 213
flint 288
flipchart 174
flip-flop 37
flipper 239, 290
float ball 61
flock 183
flood 287
floor 58, 62, 71
floor exercises 235
floor plan 261
florentine 141
floret 122
florist 110, 188
floss v 50
flours 138
flower 297
flowerbed 85, 90
flowering plant 297
flowering shrub 87
flowers 110
flu 44
flute 139, 257
fly 244, 295
fly v 211
fly-fishing 245
flysheet 266
foal 185
focus v 271
focusing knob 167
fog 287
foil 249
folder 177
foliage 110
folk music 259
follicle 20
font 177
food 118, 130, 149
food hall 105

english

english

english

english

français • english

english

english

english

english

english

english

remerciements • acknowledgments

DORLING KINDERSLEY would like to thank Tracey Miles and Christine Lacey for design assistance, Georgina Garner for editorial and administrative help, Sonia Gavira, Polly Boyd, and Cathy Meeus for editorial help, and Claire Bowers for compiling the DK picture credits.

The publisher would like to thank the following for their kind permission to reproduce their photographs:

Abbreviations key: a-above; b-below/bottom; c-center; f-far; l-left; r-right; t-top)

123RF.com: Andriy Popov 34tl; Daniel Ernst 179tc; Hongqi Zhang 24cla. 175cr; Ingvar Bjork 60c; Kobby Dagan 259c; leonardo255 269c; Liubov Vadimovna (Luba) Nel 39cla; Ljupco Smokovski 75crb; Oleksandr Marynchenko 60bl; Olga Popova 33c; oneblink 49bc; Racorn 162tl; Robert Churchill 94c; Roman Gorielov 33bc; Ruslan Kudrin 35bc, 35br; Subbotina 39cra; Sutichak Yachaingkham 39tc; Tarzhanova 37tc; Vitaly Valua 39tl; Wavebreak Media Ltd 188bl; Wilawan Khasawong 75cb; **Action Plus:** 224bc; **Alamy Images:** 154t; A.T. Willett 287bcl; Alex Segre 105ca, 105cb, 195cl; Ambrophoto 24cra; Blend Images 168cr; Cultura RM 33r; Doug Houghton 107fbr; Ekkapon Sriharun 172bl; Hugh Threlfall 35tl; 176tr; Ian Allenden 48br; Ian Dagnall (iPod is a trademark of Apple Inc., registered in the U.S. and other countries) 268tc, 270t; Ievgen Chepil 250bc; imagebroker 199tl, 249c; keith morris 178c; Martyn Evans 210b; MBI 175tl; Michael Burrell 213cra; Michael Foyle 184bl; Oleksiy Maksymenko 105tc; Paul Weston 168br; Prisma Bildagentur AG 246b; Radharc Images 197tr; RBtravel 112tl; Ruslan Kudrin 176tl; Sasa Huzjak 258t; Sergey Kravchenko 37ca; Sergio Azenha 270bc; Stanca Sanda (iPad is a trademark of Apple Inc., registered in the U.S. and other countries) 176bc; Stock Connection 287bcr; tarczas 35cr; vitaly suprun 176cl; Wavebreak Media ltd 39cl, 174b, 175tr; **Allsport/Getty Images:** 238cl; **Alvey and Towers:** 209 acr, 215bcl, 215bcr, 241cr; **Peter Anderson:** 188cbr, 271br. **Anthony Blake Photo Library:** Charlie Stebbings 114cl; John Sims 114tcl; **Andyalte:** 98tl; **apple mac computers:** 268tcr; **Arcaid:** John Edward Linden 301bl; Martine Hamilton Knight, Architects: Chapman Taylor Partners, 213cl; Richard Bryant 301br; **Argos:** 41tcl, 66cbl, 66cl, 66br, 66bcl, 69cl, 70bcl, 71t, 77tl, 269tc, 270tl; **Axiom:** Eitan Simanor 105bcr; Ian Cumming 104; Vicki Couchman 148cr; **Beken Of Cowes Ltd:** 215cbc; **Bosch:** 76tcr, 76tc, 76tcl; **Camera Press:** 38tr, 256t, 257cr; Barry J. Holmes 148tr; Jane Hanger 159cr; Mary Germanou 259bc; **Corbis:** 78b; Anna Clopet 247tr; Ariel Skelley / Blend Images 52l; Bettmann 181tl, 181br; Blue Jean Images 48bl; Bo Zauders 156t; Bob Rowan 152bl; Bob Winsett 247cbl; Brian Bailey 247br; Carl and Ann Purcell 162l; Chris Rainer 247cctl; Craig Aurness 215bl; David H.Wells 249cbr; Dennis Marsico

274bl; Dimitri Lundt 236bc; Duomo 211tl; Gail Mooney 277ccr; George Lepp 248c; Gerald Nowak 239b; Gunter Marx 248cr; Jack Hollingsworth 231bl; Jacqui Hurst 277cbr; James L. Amos 247bl, 191ctr, 220bcr; Jan Butchofsky 277cbc; Johnathan Blair 243cr; Jose F. Poblete 191br; Jose Luis Pelaez.Inc 153tc; Karl Weatherly 220bl, 247tcr; Kelly Mooney Photography 259tl; Kevin Fleming 249bc; Kevin R. Morris 105tr, 243tl, 243tc; Kim Sayer 249tcr; Lynn Goldsmith 258t; Macduff Everton 231bcl; Mark Gibson 249bl; Mark L. Stephenson 249tcl; Michael Pole 115tr; Michael S. Yamashita 247ccl; Mike King 247cbl; Neil Rabinowitz 214br; Pablo Corral 115bc; Paul A. Sounders 169br, 249cctl; Paul J. Sutton 224c, 224br; Phil Schermeister 227b, 248tr; R. W Jones 309; Richard Morrell 189bc; Rick Doyle 241ctr; Robert Holmes 97br, 277cc; Roger Ressmeyer 169tr; Russ Schleipman 229; The Purcell Team 211ctr; Vince Streano 194t; Wally McNamee 220br, 220bcl, 224bl; Wavebreak Media LTD 191bc; Yann Arhus-Bertrand 249tl; **Demetrio Carrasco / Dorling Kindersley (c) Harpy / Les Editions Casterman:** 112ccl; **Dorling Kindersley:** Banbury Museum 35c; Five Napkin Burger 152t; **Dixons:** 270cl, 270cr, 270bl, 270bcl, 270bcr, 270ccr; **Dreamstime.com:** Alexander Podshivalov 179tr, 191cr; Alexxl66 268tl; Andersastphoto 176tc; Andrey Popov 191bl; Arne9001 190tl; Chaoss 26c; Designsstock 269cl; Monkey Business Images 26clb; Paul Michael Hughes 162tr; Serghei Starus 190bc; **Education Photos:** John Walmsley 26tl; **Empics Ltd:** Adam Day 236br; Andy Heading 243c; Steve White 249cbc; **Getty Images:** 48bcl, 100t, 114bcr, 154bl, 287tr; 94tr; Don Farrall / Digital Vision 176c; Ethan Miller 270bl; Inti St Clair 179bl; Liam Norris 188br; Sean Justice / Digital Vision 24br; **Dennis Gilbert:** 106tc; **Hulsta:** 70t; **Ideal Standard Ltd:** 72r; **The Image Bank/Getty Images:** 58; **Impact Photos:** Eliza Armstrong 115cr; Philip Achache 246t; **The Interior Archive:** Henry Wilson, Alfie's Market 114bl; Luke White, Architect: David Mikhail, 59tl; Simon Upton, Architect: Phillippe Starck, St Martins Lane Hotel 100bc, 100br; **iStockphoto.com:** asterix0597 163tl; EdStock 190br; RichLegg 26bc; SorinVidis 27cr; **Jason Hawkes Aerial Photography:** 216t; **Dan Johnson:** 35r; **Kos Pictures Source:** 215cbl, 240tc, 240tr; David Williams 216b; **Lebrecht Collection:** Kate Mount 169bc; **MP Visual.com:** Mark Swallow 202t; **NASA:** 280cr, 280ccl, 281tl; **P&O Princess Cruises:** 214bl; **P A Photos:** 181br; **The Photographers' Library:** 186bl, 186bc, 186t; **Plain and Simple Kitchens:** 66t; **Powerstock Photolibrary:** 169tl, 256t, 287cc; **PunchStock:** Image Source 195tr; **Rail Images:** 208c, 208 cbl, 209br; **Red Consultancy:** Odeon cinemas 257bcr; **Redferns:** 259br; Nigel Crane 259c; **Rex**

Features: 106br, 259tc, 259tr, 259bl, 280b; Charles Ommaney 114tcr; J.F.F Whitehead 243cl; Patrick Barth 101tl; Patrick Frilet 189cbl; Scott Wiseman 287bl; **Royalty Free Images:** Getty Images/Eyewire 154bl; **Science & Society Picture Library:** Science Museum 202b; **Science Photo Library:** IBM Research 190cla; NASA 281cr; **SuperStock:** Ingram Publishing 62; Juanma Aparicio / age fotostock 172t; Nordic Photos 269tl; **Skyscan:** 168t, 182c, 298; Quick UK Ltd 212; **Sony:** 268bc; **Robert Streeter:** 154br; **Neil Sutherland:** 82tr, 83tl, 90t, 118, 188ctr, 196tl, 196tr, 299cl, 299bl; **The Travel Library:** Stuart Black 264t; **Travelex:** 97cl; **Vauxhall:** Technik 198t, 199tl, 199tr, 199cl, 199ctr, 199cctcl, 199ctcr, 199tcl, 199tcr, 200; **View Pictures:** Dennis Gilbert, Architects: ACDP Consulting, 106t; Dennis Gilbert, Chris Wilkinson Architects, 209tr; Peter Cook, Architects: Nicholas Crimshaw and partners, 208t; **Betty Walton:** 185br; **Colin Walton:** 2, 4, 7, 9, 10, 28, 42, 56, 92, 95c, 99tl, 99tcl, 102, 116, 120t, 138t, 146, 150t, 160, 170, 191cctl, 192, 218, 252, 260br, 260l, 261tr, 261c, 261cr, 271cbl, 271cbr, 271ctl, 278, 287br, 302, 401.

DK PICTURE LIBRARY:

Akhil Bahkshi; Patrick Baldwin; Geoff Brightling; British Museum; John Bulmer; Andrew Butler; Joe Cornish; Brian Cosgrove; Andy Crawford and Kit Hougton; Philip Dowell; Alistair Duncan; Gables; Bob Gathany; Norman Hollands; Kew Gardens; Peter James Kindersley; Vladimir Kozlik; Sam Lloyd; London Northern Bus Company Ltd; Tracy Morgan; David Murray and Jules Selmes; Musée Vivant du Cheval, France; Museum of Broadcast Communications; Museum of Natural History; NASA; National History Museum; Norfolk Rural Life Museum; Stephen Oliver; RNLI; Royal Ballet School; Guy Ryecart; Science Museum; Neil Setchfield; Ross Simms and the Winchcombe Folk Police Museum; Singapore Symphony Orchestra; Smart Museum of Art; Tony Souter; Erik Svensson and Jeppe Wikstrom; Sam Tree of Keygrove Marketing Ltd; Barrie Watts; Alan Williams; Jerry Young.

Additional Photography by Colin Walton.

Colin Walton would like to thank:
A&A News, Uckfield; Abbey Music, Tunbridge Wells; Arena Mens Clothing, Tunbridge Wells; Burrells of Tunbridge Wells; Gary at Di Marco's; Jeremy's Home Store, Tunbridge Wells; Noakes of Tunbridge Wells; Ottakar's, Tunbridge Wells; Selby's of Uckfield; Sevenoaks Sound and Vision; Westfield, Royal Victoria Place, Tunbridge Wells.

All other images © Dorling Kindersley
For further information see: www.dkimages.com

français • english